Myron Z. Bernstein

Kambs Publishing

To Kathy
The love of my life

Have You Been Royally Screwed?
Copyright © 2009 by Myron Z. Bernstein
Published by Kambs Publishing

For further information, please visit:
info@askmyron.net

Printed in the United States of America

Have You Been Royally Screwed?
Myron Z. Berstein

1. Title   2. Author   3. Consumer/Self-help/Business

Library of Congress Control Number: 2008909972

ISBN 10: 0-9822069-0-9
ISBN 13: 978-0-9822069-0-4

Table of Contents

Prologue

This book is for anyone who has ever felt helpless in dealing with consumer rights and the oxymoron that is called "customer service." Over the past thirty-five years, I, like many of you, have seen customer service deteriorate from talking to a nice, helpful person on the phone to a voice machine directing me to some call center halfway around the world, where I eventually end up leaving my name and number with the promise of a return call in forty-eight to seventy-two hours. Of course, if I am not around when that call comes, I have missed my golden opportunity to talk with a person and must start the cycle all over again.

Every time anyone purchases a product, it comes with a warranty. You may have noticed recently that they are now called "limited warranties" and cover really nothing. Many times, the cost of mailing the item back to the manufacturer is more than what the item costs in the first place. Yet, as limited as they may seem, there are certain rights that every consumer has to receive proper warranty service. How to make the system work is another story. Sometimes it is easier to toss the item in the trash than it is to exercise your warranty rights. The companies know it and count on that fact.

Insurance is another one of those industries designed to spin the consumer around in circles with such excessive legal terminology that you have no idea what's going on. This is an area of concern to all of us. Various policies spell out the company's position and our rights but when we try to exercise those rights, we find out that the interpretation of the document means something totally different than what we had anticipated. There is often a dichotomy between the promotional literature from the insurance company and what is actually written in the three dozen pages of the policy itself. Even the agents who sell you these policies have no idea what they really mean, but it is their job to sell you insurance and make you think they understand. It isn't until you need to use your policy that the attorneys for the insurance company put a different spin on things.

Health insurance is one of the biggest deceptions ever perpetrated upon the American public. The system is controlled by insurance lobbyists, who work on behalf of major health insurance carriers. The goal is to offer the public a sense of security. Try reading your policy, if you have one at all. You may have received an overview from the company but have never really seen the full policy itself. It is almost impossible to obtain the full policy. The health carriers work on the premise that if you don't know or understand your coverage and rights, then the interpretation of the policy is strictly up to them. How many times have we heard the term "UCR" (usual and customary rates)? Did you know that each company has different UCR rates and that those rates vary depending upon the type and quality of the policy you have with that company? There's nothing "usual and customary" about it—but that's how it is.

Have you recently gone into a store to buy a mattress? Not only are you being sold comfort and quality but a different warranty depending on how high-level your item is. These warranties are printed on a small card attached to the mattress spelling out the terms of the "limited warranty." Just try to use that warranty and it is amazing how the words on the card change from a few simple sentences to a ten-page document that you never saw at the time of purchase. Remember, you made your purchase based on the salesperson letting you know how strong the warranty was and how easy it would be if you needed service.

Sometimes there are non-written promises of expectation that come with an item or service (such as that they work properly). It is fair and reasonable to expect that these implied warranties will be honored in exchange for the hard-earned money you spent. When the need arises and everyone turns away from fulfilling those guarantees, you stand there perplexed, not knowing what to do or how to get people to fulfill those promises.

Over the years, I have personally fought against many of these issues and won. In order to protect your rights, you do not have to hire an attorney. There are certain legal rights built into small claims court or the insurance commission that protect you, the consumer. You must be tenacious and willing to take a little time to push your way into the system and make it work for you. The system is designed to help consumers but it is so complex that it often doesn't seem to work. It is amazing, though, how many people out there are willing to help you get what you deserve if you know where to go and what to ask for. The most important key I can give you is to never take no for an answer if you think you are right. This is what an attorney often does until he or she prevails for the client, so why should you be any different?

Most large corporations do not like negative publicity. Your case could become public knowledge once it gets into the courts and there are always reporters hanging around who would like something to write about, especially a human interest story. Be assertive and if all goes according to plan, large companies will want to make your problem go away.

Consumers do not always buy products and services based upon the overall quality but on the company's marketing. If you have never heard someone say, "It's all in the marketing," then you've just heard it now. Companies hire professional marketing agencies to do demographic studies and figure out the best target market for their particular product or service. We, the consumers, are being led down the path without realizing that it is being done. Just look at "designer" shirts. If a brand name, any name, is on a shirt, even if it's nobody we've ever heard of, consumers purchase it as though it were designer clothing.

Over the years, I have taken on some of the largest corporations and won. I am just like anyone else reading this book—with one difference. I have been willing to push for my rights and not just say to myself that there is nothing I can do. If companies promise me something, I expect them to deliver, nothing more and nothing less.

The purpose of this book is to demonstrate to you

that, as a consumer, you have certain inalienable rights. Each and every one of us can either lie down and let them walk all over us or take charge and stand up for what is rightly ours. I hope the information will inspire readers to stop letting large companies, or even little ones, make us feel like they are doing us a favor by allowing us to purchase their goods and services.

Chapter 1

Why Let Mattress Stores Ruin Your Sleep?

The best sales gimmicks I have seen, next to those employed by used car dealers, are those of discount mattress stores. The ads are wonderful: two-for-one sales, buy one at full price and get the other at half price, buy on a specific day and get a free set of sheets or installation, and on and on. And the manufacturer's warranties! Read them sometime… they promise the consumer the world without really promising anything.

Case One: Returning a Mattress

A number of years ago, I decided to purchase a new mattress set. The salesperson was really effective and impressed me with the warranty, like when you're buying a new car and the salesperson says that you are getting the best warranty in the industry and that the car will hold its value. Sometimes I think salespeople go home at night and saw off their growing noses, like Pinocchio. They are so used to using the same sales pitch to make a living that they must begin to believe it themselves.

My new mattress set came and we were thrilled; in fact, everything was great for the first two or three years. Then we began to have a few problems but turned the mattress over according to the instructions so as not to void our ten-year limited warranty. Still, we started to notice that no matter how we turned the mattress, it was leaning to one side and sagging. My wife weighed a grand total of 110 pounds and I was at about 167, so an average mattress should have more than withstood our weight.

I called the manufacturer's hot line and asked for service under the warranty. My information was taken and I was told I'd receive a call from their area service representative shortly (which, as we know, could mean one to three months if you don't ask for a specific time). The call came and the representative stopped by my house to look at the problem.

About ten days later, I received a letter indicating that the service technician could not find any problem; therefore, nothing would be done under the warranty. I called the company again and was told I'd have to wait another six months before restarting the process (though there was nothing about that mentioned in my warranty).

So here's your choice: sleep in a sagging bed for six more months or become the aggressor and go after your rights. Many consumers would just accept the company standards and either wait half a year or go out and buy a new bed, chalking it up to experience. But let me demonstrate how I handled the situation.

First, I found out how to file a claim in small claims court. The court mailed me the papers and for a whole fourteen dollars, I was underway. Suing a large corporation will get you nowhere. You must search the state records to locate the name of the resident agent. Once you have that information, it will be this person you want to start action against (the actual person, not the nameless corporation). Sometimes you will find one corporation hiding behind another, but ultimately there is a resident agent.

Well, I did just that, filing my claim for the return of the bed and asking the court for my money back since I felt the company was not living up to its warranty. (You do not need an attorney to do this; simply write this information out carefully and submit it to the court.)

There are two ways in which the court can notify the resident agent of the case: by certified mail or by using a sheriff for the service. I always use a sheriff since it means someone will show up in uniform to serve the agent. This is a great form of intimidation and may bring you a quick settlement.

As the day of the hearing got closer, I received a call from the parent corporation to settle the matter. Let's figure out why they called: My going to court would cost me a few hours of my day, but it would cost the company a few thousand dollars to hire a local attorney, even to only try to get the case dismissed. The winner in the end is you, the consumer.

The result was that I received full credit for my original purchase price of the mattress. I decided to take that money and go to the store, this time to pick out a top-of-the-line set with an even longer and stronger warranty. I put extra money towards the purchase and was so pleased with the new set that I told my son and his wife to buy the same one for their new home. Sweet dreams? No, another nightmare.

Case Two: The Second Mattress

So here we go again. After two and a half years, it became evident that this top-of-the-line set was not going to last as long as I expected. We had two sags in the right and left sides of the bed, so I called the company and requested an adjuster come look at it. (My son was having the same problem with the exact same mattress in his home.)

The adjuster put a laser light across the bed and noted that the sag was one and a quarter inches on one side and one and seven-sixteenths of an inch on the other. According to the written terms of the warranty, if the bed sagged an inch and a half or more, a new replacement would be given.

A letter came about ten days later indicating that my mattress did not meet the criteria to warrant a replacement. Our sags did not meet their standards. We were off by less than a quarter-inch. I reread the warranty and realized that it didn't specify if the measurement was to be taken with or without a person in the bed.

I called the manufacturer's corporate office and talked with a customer service representative, who said that they leave it up to the individual store to handle the warranty. I replied that my warranty was with the company, not the store, and pointed out that it was unclear as to whether the bed was to be occupied or not during measurement. She said, "Of course, it means empty" and should be assumed as such, but if I had an issue with that, I'd have to go back to the store in six months. My wife was nearing back surgery and I needed to do something. I put boards under the bed, which helped for a while, but I was really angry because my only recourse was to throw the mattress out and buy something new again. Or was it?

Back to the courts I went. I filed a claim against the resident agent and sent a sheriff to serve the notice of a court date. That date came and went and neither the resident agent nor an attorney for the company ever showed. The entire amount of the set and the court fees were awarded in my favor by the judge, and the court would send notice of the ruling to the resident agent, who had thirty days to contest (which he did not).

At the end of the thirty days, I had to go back to court to file a writ of execution to be served by the sheriff. (This told the resident agent that I intended to collect using the remedies allowed by my state.) In Maryland, I can garnish wages or attach bank accounts. After forty-five days, if the resident agent or an attorney for the corporation does not do anything, I can go back to the judge to request that all the assets of the corporation and all of their checking accounts be identified at the next meeting set by the court so that I can attach some entity to receive my funds. This means that the company would have to show me all of its corporate records, accounts and other assets.

This is the second time I had to go this far for my consumer rights. The next meeting assigned by the court came and went, and still nobody showed up to verify the assets. As a result, the judge issued a bench warrant for the arrest of the resident agent for defying a direct court order.

Forty-eight hours later, I received a call from an attorney for the company indicating that this was the first he had heard of my claim. They wanted to settle immediately for all court costs and the original price of the mattress set. I was at a crossroads: accept the payment or insist on being paid for the time it took me to get to this point. I told the attorney that I would release them totally if I received the cost of the set, court costs and $1,000 for my time. Not surprisingly, he rejected the $1,000.

I could accept everything without these additional damages or refuse and tell him I'd see him in court (which would mean thousands of dollars for the company to send its attorney to my area). Since it had taken ten months to get to this point, I had already bought a new mattress and thrown out the old one; therefore, I could no longer prove its inferior quality. So I accepted the original cost of the mattress set plus court costs with no additional payment.

Sometimes it is best to take your money and run—but you don't ever have to take broken guarantees and poor quality lying down!

Chapter 2

The Dangers of Discount Airline Tickets

Case One: Online Discount Tickets

Buying tickets with one of those supposedly cheap online services could turn out to be more than you bargained for.

I booked some tickets on a flight to Europe and it seemed easy enough. Even though I did it online, I had to call to make a few alternative arrangements with a customer service agent, who suggested I buy insurance to cover any and all cancellations, just in case. This sounded like a smart idea so I took the advice.

Sure enough, a few weeks went by and I had to cancel the trip. First, I called the customer service line and talked to someone who barely spoke English. I was informed that I could exchange the tickets but had to send them back via registered mail, which was extremely expensive, but I had no choice.

Four days later I received a tracking confirmation that the tickets had indeed arrived. I called the customer service line and had to explain the whole story to another representative all over again. This person put me on hold for a few minutes then came back to tell me that I'd have to talk with the exchange department. I was transferred to a totally different person and had to repeat the same story. I was again put on hold for another four or five minutes before the voice came back to say that they hadn't received the tickets and that I must mail them back first.

Sighing, I explained how I already did that and, according to the tracking record, the tickets had arrived and were signed for some twelve hours earlier by someone in the company. Again I was placed on hold before being told that the tickets couldn't be located and that I should call back the next day.

The following day, I called again. The first customer service person put me on a long, extended hold twice, while either learning the English language or going out for coffee. Finally, I was told that the exchange fee was $245 per ticket, plus whatever the difference in airfare was for the new booking. I told the agent that I had already contacted the airline directly about this matter and they said it would only cost $135. Naturally, the next words I heard were, "Please hold."

This time the agent returned with the information that the tickets were non-exchangeable and that I could either use them or throw them away. One minute it was one thing and the next, something else. I asked about using the insurance policy and was told to call the insurance company directly, even though I bought the policy through the ticket agent.

Now the story starts to change. I called the insurance company only to find out that this policy covered my death or illness or that of a family member. Oh, and it also covered cancellation—in the case that my house burned down!

So I called the airline directly and the reservation agent offered me one half the value of my original ticket to apply to the fare for the new ticket. This cost far less than exchanging it through the "cheap" Internet service, which had also changed its tune earlier and said the tickets were non-exchangeable.

Fine. So now I changed my tickets. But I was still angry with the online company. Not only was I sold insurance that was different than described but I was also told I couldn't exchange tickets that were supposed to be exchangeable—and, boy, do I dislike that old "bait and switch" technique.

I contacted my credit card company, explaining the

details of what had transpired, and they immediately reversed the charges and started a full investigation. However, remember that credit card companies are really working for the merchant, not for the consumer, no matter how comfortable they make you feel. It's simple finance: The fees they receive from the merchant are higher than those from the customer.

It took about six weeks for the investigation to be completed. The credit card company sent me all the paperwork they had received supporting the merchant's claim and indicated that it had been a fair transaction. If that ever happens to you, don't accept it. Write back to the credit card company and continue to dispute the false claims and actions of the merchant.

The final step to bring this to a close is to threaten legal action not only against the merchant but also against the credit card company (especially in my case, since I had proof that the Internet travel site had defrauded me). I had the upper hand. All I had to do was be willing to sue the proper person in my local court; these two companies would have to hire attorneys to fight the action.

Sure, it would be easier for me to simply pay the charges and forget it, but that is exactly what they were counting on. The credit card companies figured I would pay my bill so that they wouldn't put any type of hit on my credit report, which takes some time and trouble to reverse, even if I am in the right. The government standards about fair credit reporting are really a farce, and it could take months and even years for me to successfully fight the action. It isn't as scary as they intend it to sound.

The end result for me was that the credit card company requested the Internet travel site to further verify its position in light of the material I sent. When they couldn't, the charges were permanently reversed and the matter was settled in my favor. Online companies may try to hide behind an anonymous computer screen, but they are just as responsible to their customers as brick and mortar stores.

Chapter 3

Hassles With the Health Industry

Most of us believe that by having health insurance, we are covered all the way. Like any other insurance company out there, health insurance carriers paint you and your employer a picture of just how good their coverage is. Naturally, they hide the negatives and don't mention the things that are not covered (found under "Exclusions"). Health insurance carriers do not clarify which drugs are or are not in their formulary and they do not go into specifics about which procedures are considered "experimental" or which services are not deemed "medically necessary." There are no guidelines in the industry; each of these categories is determined by the company itself.

Always remember that you have certain rights and options available to you as a consumer, even when it comes to health coverage. If you think your company is not living up to its agreed upon promises, pursue your complaint. Insurance companies will often respond by sending you a note saying that you have the right to write a letter of appeal, but that appeal is reviewed by people working for the insurance company! I can almost guarantee that ninety-nine percent of appeals are refused. After all, do you think the insurance company likes giving away money? Their game is to wear you out until you throw your hands in the air, figuring you can't fight city hall, so to speak.

Insurance companies probably save millions in payouts by simply making a few processing 'mistakes' on a large percentage of claims or by denying claims as not being medically necessary. The insured often reads the explanation of benefits form and simply accepts that "it is what it is." They rarely question the charges or payments and take it all on blind faith. I suggest you look at your explanation of benefits very carefully and review it along with the terms of your policy. It is amazing what errors you will find.

Even though the insurance company's customer service center representatives are trained to act like your best friends, they are not. They work for the company, not for you, and will often politely explain that your policy doesn't cover a particular service or that service is being processed under UCR (usual and customary rates). But different insurance companies have different UCR, so it is in your best interest to ask for a list of the relative values and the dollar amounts that are attached.

I'll give you a few examples of how situations that at first seemed like a lost cause can turn into a positive result if you know how to go after the health insurance companies and go for what you believe is right.

Case One: X-Ray Studies

Recently, I ventured into a study called a cardiac calcium count. Even though you as a consumer (as well as your doctor) may think this is a great test, many insurance companies term it "experimental." Therefore, they will not want to pay for it. It takes insurance companies between three and five years to fit many new tests into their actuarial tables, so until that happens, these tests remain "experimental."

Knowing this, I called various hospitals to find out which, if any, would take payment through insurance, if it were available. I found one that considered the test a form of CT scan; therefore, they would bill my insurance and accept whatever the company offered as full payment. But there was one problem: The person who told me this on the phone, who was in charge of making appointments, was not really trained to know how the system works. If some services were not covered, that person had no idea (by the way, the billing department has no idea, either).

When the day came, I went to the hospital and had my scan. The billing was filed with my insurance company and, about three weeks later, they paid the charge using a contracted price with the hospital.

About a month after that, I received a bill from a radiology group for the reading portion of the scan. It stated that the procedure was "experimental" so the insurance company would not pay. However, when I had initially called the hospital, I was told it was covered. At no time did anyone indicate that only taking the scan was covered, not reading it. They didn't even tell me that the reading would be performed by a radiology group that was not really part of the hospital. In fact, most patients would not even know to ask that question.

So I called the hospital's billing department, which had a different take than the person who originally made the appointment and assured me I was covered. The billing department said that I, the patient, should have understood that the radiologists were separate from the hospital and that I was expected to pay them the going rate.

This left me with a choice: refuse to pay the radiology

group and file an appeal with the administrator of the hospital based upon what I was originally told, or file a complaint with my state insurance commissioner and consumer protection agency. The latter is a better option because it's independent of the hospital.

If you do ever file with these agencies, make sure you stay on top of them or they will often try to sweep your case under the carpet, which creates less work for them. The insurance commission may side with the insurance company or the hospital at first, but don't accept this in the first round. Keep fighting and you are sure to prevail.

In this case, however, I decided to handle it in a different way. I was in medicine for my entire career so I understood the dilemma with the radiologists, but you can do the same. Explain to the billing department of the radiology group that you were told by the hospital that the service was all-inclusive, so you are not obligated to pay them. Ask them to get their payment from the hospital since they made the mistake. The person you are talking to will probably be surprised and balk. Here is the solution.

When a service is not covered by insurance, you, the consumer, are being charged the most that the doctor can charge for that service. This is the great American rip-off. Doctors have negotiated fees with companies—but with the consumer, the sky's the limit!

Tell the radiology billing person that you'd be willing to pay the contracted price that the group would have received from Medicare, even if you are not of Medicare age. Medicare has established a level of fees that most insurance companies follow today. Under federal law, no doctor is permitted to charge any patient, even within his or her own family, less than the rate received from Medicare for a similar service.

Now you have left *them* with a choice: you'll pay the doctors nothing and they will have to ask the hospital for their fee, or you'll pay the fee that they would receive from Medicare. In my case, as in most cases, I received a call back that the radiology group changed their fee from $183 all the way down to $60. I paid this amount and it was a win-win for both of us.

Case Two: Disability Insurance

Disability insurance is another one of those unknowns. When you purchase these policies, the company promises you the world, until it is time to pay out. Many policies written twenty to thirty years ago had more liberal payouts than those of today. Always read your new policy carefully and if you need help understanding what you bought, ask a professional. The legal language is written in a very ambiguous way so that it will be open to interpretation when necessary. These disability insurance companies will try to interpret the policy in their best interests, not yours. They will even try to apply newer policy language to older policies by manipulating the wording. Don't let them get away with it.

During my career, I had two occasions to use my disability policy. The first was quite a few years ago when I was in my mid-forties. I thought it would be a very simple process and I applied with the usual disability form. The first thing I received was a letter requesting my tax returns for two years and account statements in order to review my level of disability. I was confined to my house so I could gather the information rather easily. I sent them the tax forms pertaining to me; my wife's were not their business.

About four weeks later, I received another letter requesting *all* of my tax forms (notice that it 'only' took four weeks for them to respond to me). At that point, I still had no money coming in and they knew it. I called the company and told them that they were only entitled to my tax reports and not the joint filings, since other parts of my taxes were involved with my wife's company. This went back and forth for weeks until I had an attorney call them. Then they agreed to only accept my records.

These companies will do anything to badger you into thinking that if you do not comply with their every request, right or wrong, you will not receive benefits. Don't believe it for a minute. You have rights—and the right to privacy is among the most important. You are obligated to give them only what is truly necessary and nothing more.

They paid my disability but not without a fight. It took them sixteen weeks to make the full payment—and the insurance company was making money on *my* money all that time by keeping it in the bank as long as they could.

I had a relapse a few months later and the company required the process to start all over since it was outside the six-month period to be considered part of the same occurrence. Naturally, they started to fight about making the payments again. This time I was requesting a "residual" payment since I could work some of the time.

Weeks went by and one day I received a call from the company's regional field representative, who came to visit me in my home. He produced a video that was made by a private investigator to observe my movements over the past three weeks. This tape showed me lifting some groceries into the trunk of my car, and the company felt that since my problem was with a cervical disc, I should not have been lifting anything. That was not true; my therapist assured me I could lift light things safely if I bent a certain way.

The representative said that the company wanted to return all my years of premium payments and they would cancel my policy, indicating that my records would "disappear." I, of course, would be free to buy insurance from another company. This sounded too easy to be true. So, of course, it wasn't. Any insurance or disability record is logged in a national databank. Company records could disappear, but not those in the databank. Simply put, what they wanted me to commit was insurance fraud by not letting a new company know that I ever had my original policy. Fortunately, I had a hidden tape recorder running the whole time.

I gave the tape to my attorney and he approached the corporate level of the insurance company with the information that was exchanged at my home. You better believe that someone was fired! Up to then, the company owed me over a year and a half of payments. I not only wanted those payments but interest, court costs and attorney's fees. They knew I was right so they quickly agreed.

Even in the case of disability payments, I had the ability to get what you deserve.

Case Three: Final Disability

In my later years, a disc in my lower back popped out of place and this put me off my feet for months. I applied for disability, but this time they were much easier on me and agreed to accept only the necessary paperwork. I guess they learned that I couldn't be intimidated into giving them more than they were entitled to.

Everything went well until I returned to work part-time and requested residual payments. The insurance company kept asking me for more and more of my company papers, which got annoying. They were trying to find a way to cut off my payments by using the total company profits to determine the base of my residual payments. Many people would take this as gospel, but it is wrong. Read the wording of your policy carefully and remember that the company will try to interpret a twenty-year-old policy in their best interest by using the phrasing of newer policies. That is exactly what they tried to do with me.

While we fought for months, they continued making my payments, indicating that if they were found right, I would have to return the money. It took some time and many letters for the insurance company to understand that the gross revenue of my practice was also based upon two other partners. In order to fairly determine my loss for residual, they had to take my partners' production out of the equation and concentrate only on my production and share of the expenses, which was one-third of the total. That clearly showed my loss of income.

Eventually, this disability cost me the loss of my partnership and I could not find a job doing what I did before because of my age. My insurance company was also in a bind since they never had this type of situation before. I started to negotiate a buy-out of my policy since it would be in both of our best interests.

A representative from the company called to work with me, trying to become my best friend—but I kept in mind that he worked for the company. What it came down to was an equation of the future value of my policy, the government average death age for someone of my generation, and a percentage of that number. We tried numerous times, but could not reach an agreement. The company was trying to pay out as little money as it possibly could.

It was in my best interest to stop talking to my new "best friend" and hire an attorney to negotiate the deal, indicating that I'd be willing to go to court. I didn't care what it would cost; I was willing to take on the company in a fair fight. As we got closer to a court date, they caved in and agreed to pay me out at a reasonable rate based upon my financial consultant's computation of the numbers.

Sometimes even the giants know when the little guy is going to win!

Case Four: Health Insurance and the Hospital

Your health insurance company will do anything it can to make you think that certain things are your financial responsibility and not theirs. Again, read your policy and review your explanation of benefits to make sure you receive everything they owe you.

I recently had the unfortunate experience of spending three days in a local hospital after surgery. I was comfortable that I understood my medical coverage, since I had been in that industry for over thirty years, and, at first, everything went fine. I paid my deductibles according to schedule, but then received a bill from the hospital. To my surprise, I had a few hundred dollars remaining on my bill, which was not covered by insurance.

Think about it: If the insurance company leaves the consumer with a few hundred dollars of out-of-pocket expenses and they do this with a million customers, that saves them an extra half a billion dollars a year. When you, the insured, see a hospital bill for thousands of dollars and only a few hundred is termed "your responsibility," well, naturally it seems so small that you pay it. Check the terms of your policy very carefully. You'll be amazed how many things were not paid correctly. The amount I owed was not only incorrect, but the hospital owed me my deductible!

It was an uphill battle to prove my point. Your insurance company will do everything to run interference and make you interpret the terms of the policy in their best interest.

At first I called the insurance company and tried to show them logically how they did not pay according to the letter of my policy. The person I spoke to in customer service was trained to say the minimal amount and just repeat that this "is the way your policy reads" (rest assured that person has no idea what the actual terms of your policy are). Insurance companies do not respond to logic. They are there to move you on and in most cases, consumers will simply accept what they say and go away. I am not one of them.

By the third time I called, I found a customer service representative who agreed with me on one of the eight items. She said it would be reviewed and should probably change. Oh, it was reviewed all right! No surprise, they stood their ground. Remember, these reviews are handled by an insurance company employee, not an independent auditor.

So I filed an appeal according to the company standards. In the appeal, I explained my position and why I thought they were wrong, and I sent additional documentation from my policy to verify my claim. I admit that I expected this to be an exercise in futility, which it was. Six weeks later I received a response trying to convince me that the terms of my policy had changed midstream.

I could not accept that statement. I bought that policy through my employer and if there had been a change, it should have come with next year's policy. So, do you think I did what they told me or hired an attorney for thousands of dollars just to save a few hundred on the bill and prove myself right? Neither, of course. I simply used the resources available to do it myself, which is something you should always look into.

I took the matter to the state insurance commission. After about four weeks, I received a letter telling me that since it was a company-funded policy, the insurance company only acts as the administrator. I was advised that this issue came under ERISA (the Employment Retirement Income Security Act), so I contacted the Department of Labor, which governs ERISA regulations.

The Department of Labor said that I needed to talk with the labor office in the region where my employer was located. So I called that office in the Midwest and about two days later, got a call back from an attorney representing the Department of Labor. After a lengthy discussion, I had the information and ammunition I needed to move forward.

I sent a letter to the human resources department of the corporate office of my employer, and they told me to file an appeal with the insurance division of the department. Phew! Here we go again. I filed an appeal with all the paperwork attached and waited five weeks for what turned out to be a negative response.

Don't stop there! In a situation like this, keep pressing the issue over and over again. One of the important moves I made was to let the HR department of the insurance company know that I was filing a grievance with ERISA. If my position proved correct and the policy had been changed midstream, it could overturn the entire program and cause them massive problems. Sooner or later, you, too, will get the attention of someone important instead of a lower-level pencil pusher.

Finally, my case got into the hands of the right person. While the front guard had tried their best to make me go away, the head of the department did not. I immediately received a telephone call from the director stating that I was correct and her staff was totally wrong. She said that under the program, as I had read it, I was entitled to a greater payment than I had received and that my original policy had never been changed. It seems that the insurance administrator was the one using totally new guidelines for payments, which was saving the company thousands of dollars, but the employees didn't really know anything about it. The director agreed that under ERISA regulations, the employer could not change the program in the middle of the year.

Since I had paid the hospital out of pocket, she informed me that the entire amount would reach me from the insurance carrier in forty-eight hours and this would include the deductible that was to be returned under the policy terms.

As you can see, sometimes the lower-level people in a company are making decisions without being fully informed. By staying on their case, you can get your problem into the hands of someone who really knows and understands the situation. Be polite but be aggressive and assertive. The system is designed to get consumers hooked into buying a company's services then they make you feel that they are doing you a favor by allowing you to use even a portion of those services that you paid for. They try to make you think that you cannot fight the system. But I just showed you that you can.

Case Five: Are You the Doctor?

A few years ago, I was having chest pains so I went to the emergency room thinking the worst. After some basic testing and lab studies, it was determined that I had strained a muscle between the ribs. What a fortunate day: It wasn't a heart attack and was quite a minor case. So what could the problem be?

The emergency room submitted their billing and my insurance decided to deny payment. Their reason was that it wasn't a necessary visit since I was not having a heart attack. They said I should have gone to my family physician first, which was complete lunacy on their part.

Naturally, I did not accept the insurance company's logic lying down. I called their customer service department and was given the same line of bull over the phone; they wouldn't back down, no matter what I had to say. In this case, my hands were tied: either get an attorney or call the state insurance commission.

I called my state insurance commission and filed an appropriate form to request an arbitration hearing. My reasoning was that when chest pain strikes, one should immediately respond by getting to the emergency room, especially since a heart attack is a silent killer.

The arbitration date was set but the insurance company reviewed the complaint to the appeal board beforehand. A higher-level employee (who obviously got his job through intelligence) agreed that it was not up to me to determine my diagnosis before deciding if I should see my doctor or go to the emergency room.

Again, this was another problem caused by the people in customer service who are trained to repeat what someone had taught them to say in order to avoid the company having to pay the customer's claim. In my case, did they really think saving eleven hundred dollars was worth asking me to risk my life?

It's obvious that consumers need to look after their own best interests. Health insurance companies sure as hell aren't going to do it for you.

Chapter 4

Going Up Against the Big Guys— Computer Companies and Home Goods Stores

One of my biggest pet peeves is dealing with customer service. Customer service is an oxymoron. Have you ever made a call to a customer service line, gone through various menu options then found yourself stuck in a holding pattern? So you sit and sit and sit until one of two things happens: Someone actually answers or the line clicks off and a familiar dial tone returns.

You think it may be a problem with your phone so you call again and the same thing happens: click and a dial tone. I've noticed that this is especially common within thirty minutes of the customer service department closing for the day. Don't be discouraged. The company you are calling is most likely doing this on purpose. The customer service line could be flooded with calls so they drop some to lighten the load in hopes that the disgruntled consumers won't call back. Or, as I have mentioned, it's almost quitting time and they don't want to get stuck dealing with you.

Sometimes there is a way to get through anyway. Call the number back and push a totally different option than you normally would, like the sales extension. Someone will always be willing to answer that line since sales are never refused, even if it is the end of the day or they are too busy.

Another scenario is that someone actually answers the phone on the routing you want. You talk to a person, most likely not in the United States. When you finally explain your problem, the person on the other end responds with an accent or dialect that is often hard to understand or says, "I am really sorry" but offers no solution.

When that happens to me, I usually respond, "I know you're sorry, but what are you going to do to rectify the situation?" Again, the response is, "I am really sorry." Again you explain your problem, and again you hear how sorry they are. These people are taught to listen, be apologetic, and never really do anything to help.

Consumers need to figure out a strategy to get some action. Ask for a supervisor. In some cases that person will get on the phone and in other cases you will be told that the supervisors are busy and will have to call you back. If the latter happens, always ask when you should expect to receive the return call. Pin them down to a specific time if you can. What is happening here is that the customer service person may be on a time limit per call and needs to get you off the phone. Once, a customer service person I was speaking to explained that he had to get me off the phone in five minutes or he could lose his job. He said that he would have to go to the supervisor to get an over-ride to stay on the phone for another fifteen minutes. I found this extremely interesting since I never knew this was happening in the industry.

Now it is your turn to become defensive by being aggressive and turning the tables. Remember, sometimes the best defense is a strong offense. If you were "acciden-tally" disconnected, call the customer service department anywhere from three to five times per day until someone finally makes a decision to act upon your request.

Case One: Computers

One of the best stories I can relate is dealing with one of those major computer manufacturing companies. When I bought the computer, the company wanted to sell me a three-year, in-home service contract for some ridiculous amount of money. Like most people, I want to protect my investment, knowing that technology breaks easily, so I go ahead and purchase the warranty. It sounds great on paper—until the first time you have to use it.

First, I called technical support and the response was quite quick. The overseas technician told me to get all the discs that came with the computer. Next, we started the process of troubleshooting everything to find the problem. I was informed that this takes time and that we could be on the phone for more than an hour.

"Hold on a minute," I exclaimed. "I purchased in-home service." The technician then explained that they would not send someone to my home until he determined the problem. I told him that my time was worth much more per hour than the cost of this in-home contract. Again, I was informed that I could not get any in-home service until the problem was figured out over the phone. Interesting that this wasn't explained to me when I bought the extended service contract.

I finally exploded and told the tech person to get me a "stupidvisor" since I was being insulted. Did they think I was so stupid that I'd pay for in-home coverage that I couldn't get until I spent *my* time helping to fix the computer they sold me? I didn't hesitate to inform him that I intended to bring legal action to fulfill my warranty rights. Of course, I really had no idea what action I could take, but neither did the person I was talking to.

The next business day, I was on the phone with the salesperson who originally sold me the equipment. For the first time, he informed me about the limits of in-home service. I let him know that I was quite willing to sit on the phone with technical support but I needed to know exactly where to send *my* bill for my time and labor. This usually throws them for a loop or they think I'm crazy. It's important not to say another word—the next person who talks usually loses. And it's often the sales-person who starts to stammer since they haven't been trained how to respond to this.

In this case, the computer salesperson replied that the company doesn't pay me for my time. I informed him that I prepaid for their service and since I'm expected to be part of that service team, I intended to get paid. The next thing I knew, my call was escalated up the ladder to a higher authority.

I explained my situation again, concluding that I should get paid if the company expected me to spend an hour on the phone fixing the problem. By now, they were getting annoyed with me and rightly so. That was exactly what I was attempting to accomplish. In some cases, I am elevated to an even higher level because nobody can believe what I am saying and I don't let up.

The end result is generally one of two solutions: I am told I can send the items back at their expense and someone will handle the problem at the service center or I can sit on the phone and help troubleshoot the unit. Naturally, I elect to send the unit back as long as they are paying for two-way mailing.

Another trick is to explain that you are computer illiterate. Every time the technician asks you a question, make it seem as though you are having difficulty understanding what he or she is requesting you to do. After a while, the technician will become frustrated with your inability to help solve the problem and will ask the supervisor permission to send someone to your house to troubleshoot it for you. Sometimes it is smart to play dumb!

Case Two: Hot Water Heaters

Have you ever had a problem with one of those super hardware stores? Well, I have a few horror stories and some solutions to get what you paid for. I purchased a product with store installation. They made it sound so simple, but many times what seems simple on the surface might not be your best option. The labor cost is usually split between the store and the person performing the installation, so you would think that the store would obtain the best quality labor. Much too often, though, the labor is not only cheap but poor quality. I will demonstrate how to deal with these companies and the problems and headaches they bestow upon each of their customers.

A few years ago I purchased a hot water heater from one of the large superstores with what I thought was a reasonable installation cost. Two days later I received a call from the plumber that he had the unit and could install it the next day, so we set up a time.

Upon arrival, the plumber informed me that the terms of the installation are what the store calls "normal installation." Could someone please define what "normal installation" means? No one at the store could. As he spoke, I realized that this gentleman was as drunk as a skunk, even though it was only ten in the morning.

He started working and, after a few minutes, informed me that the valve just above the heater wouldn't shut off all the way. He could replace it but that wasn't part of the normal installation. He further explained that according to some new code, I must have a four-inch flue. My old heater had a three-inch adapter going into a four-inch flu leading to the roof, which apparently wasn't good enough. He then proceeded to quote me the cost of replacing the shut-off valve and changing the adapter to the larger one. It was amazing how my labor cost just doubled!

I asked him to wait while I called the store's customer service desk to define "normal installation." I was informed that what he said was correct and that these items were not part of normal installation. Understand that he had to disconnect the flue anyway so putting in a four-inch section of pipe would require the same effort and labor as putting my original flue back together. It would mean only one extra solder joint to install the new cut-off valve, which would take all of thirty seconds. But my old unit was now removed so he thought I was stuck. And most people would have stood there with no choice but to proceed as he explained since they were already past the point of no return. So what is a person to do?

First, try negotiating with the plumber to simply pay for the two parts, which actually cost about fifteen dollars, and offer him a few bucks for his effort. Knowing he had me backed against a wall, he said he couldn't do that since he would lose his relationship with the store (like someone would really find out!). I knew that he was an independent contractor, though, and not an employee of the store.

I don't like to be ripped off so I told him to leave. He was flabbergasted that I would fire him at this stage of the installation, but he had already brought my new unit inside the house, which is an important point for me since the item I paid for was now on my property.

The next step is to call the store and inform customer service that you want to talk to the manager. In most large companies, the actual store manager will never talk to the "little people" (also known as "customers"), so you will be handed off to what is called the "MOD," or the manager of the day. Inform this person that you have your heater but you tossed the plumber out the door because you do not like to be taken for a ride. Insist on an immediate replacement since the old heater is gone and the water is off in the entire house.

In some cases, a manager will give you his or her condolences then offer to send another installer who will complete the job, including the cost of the two parts. They think they are doing this to keep the customer happy but, after all, isn't this what you expect in the first place from the term "normal installation"?

In other cases, the MOD may indicate that what the plumber stated was correct and there is nothing that can be done. My solution to this is to let them know you are reversing the installation charge on your credit card and will call in another plumber for about the same cost to complete the installation. Let the MOD know that you will bring this situation to the attention of the corporate office (especially in a situation like mine, when the plumber was drunk upon arriving at the house).

Call the corporate customer service number and explain your plight. Naturally, this customer service employee will apologize profusely but usually has no solution. You are talking to someone who has been trained to be polite at all times but who has also been trained to spin you back to the store manager.

Now, pick up the speed a little more. Ask if this conversation is being recorded for quality control, which it most likely is. Inform the customer service person that you not only intend to report the store to the consumer protection agency in your state but that you also intend to file a complaint with the licensing division in your area, not only against the plumber but against the store's contractor's license. This usually gets their attention.

Usually within an hour of hanging up, the manager from the local store will contact you to offer a resolution by sending someone else to finish the installation immediately and give you the parts. I have found that the store will also give you full credit for the installation in return for all your trouble.

Always be prepared to follow through on your threats. If nothing positive happens, complete the installation with your own person and notify your credit card to reverse the labor costs. In the meantime, file a complaint with the consumer protection agency in your state, not the Better Business Bureau. Also file a complaint with the division that regulates the contractor's licenses in your area or county. When the store has a choice to hire an attorney to answer the complaint, which takes time and money, they will instead decide to give you what you were entitled to from the beginning. The call will come from the manager of the store. Don't be bashful; let the manager know what the store has put you through by not taking care of the problem in a businesslike manner. The end result will probably be that the heater will be free and the labor charge to your own plumber will be given back to you directly from the store.

Why would such a large store do this? Well, one possibility is that it is more costly for them to answer the complaint or maybe they don't want the negative publicity it could bring. But the real reason is that it isn't very often that someone takes a stand and is willing to strike back in the right way to get what they deserve.

Case Three: Countertop Installation

Here is a case in which a large home store offered a great sale price for granite counters with installation. It sounded like a good deal. The price was low, the installation was free and the major company personally guaranteed the work, even though it was given to a subcontractor.

The deposit is given, the granite is selected and the first stage of installation is about to begin. The contractor comes to the house to measure and does an actual cardboard layout. Now all I have to do is wait a few weeks until the call comes for final installation.

The day of installation arrives; the company sends in four people to handle the job since the granite is so heavy. The sink is to be cut out at the last minute and installed under the granite. Wait a minute—no one has deter-mined how the plumbing would be reconnected again. Was the major home store supposed to take care of it or what?

Well, it turns out that both the salesperson at the store and I, the consumer, had failed to figure that into the equation, too. So it seemed as though I was going to have a really nice granite countertop with a new under-mount sink that would not be functional. What to do?

Actually, in this case, I had the upper hand. The counter was installed and I had full possession of the product. I called the home goods store and got the customer service division on the phone, and explained the dilemma in detail. I was told that it was my respon-sibility; most people would simply agree and take it on the chin.

I say, don't stand for it. I was sold a complete job by the home store and even though they might have subcon-tracted it to their preferred contractor, I had rights. The workers unhooked my old sink so I'd expect them to hook up the new one. I explained to the person in customer service that I would stop the payment on my credit card with a dispute until the company agreed to own up to their full responsibility and complete the installation of the faucet and drain for the sink.

Next, I asked to speak to a store manager. In most

cases, manager will not get on the phone since their job is to sit in their little office and give directions for some other person in the store to handle the problem. I always get the name of the store manager from the customer employee with whom I speak.

It is amazing what a simple certified letter to the store manager will do to help get the problem resolved. I am not going to go without plumbing while trying to get my problem resolved. I often hire and pay someone to complete the job while stating my case in detail in the letter to the manager. When I sign the letter, I put a "cc" at the bottom showing that I sent a copy to my attorney and the state consumer protection agency, even if I really didn't.

It usually takes about twenty-four hours after the manager receives the letter for me to get a phone call. The parent company does not want bad community publicity, especially with consumer protection. The manager will now do whatever it takes to rectify the problem. Don't be afraid to be aggressive enough to stand up for yourself. I would venture to guess that out of every ten people in this situation, only one would be aggressive in their approach and get the desired results.

Now the store will indicate that they will send out one of their subcontracted plumbers to fix the problem and complete the job. Ask the manager if she really thought you'd leave the plumbing unhooked for almost two weeks—or if she'd live without the use of her kitchen for that long without getting it fixed. Naturally, the answer is no. What I did in my case was put the manager in my shoes and make her see the situation from my side.

It was now safe to let the manager know that I had already had the sink connected using my own plumber, since I'd had no other choice in the matter. I asked the manager to pay for that plumbing invoice either with a direct check or by putting the credit on my credit card. I have been reimbursed both ways—and it seems to work every time.

Think this counter installation problem is over? Think again. A few weeks later, I noticed a chip in the corner, which had obviously happened during the cutting process. The manufacturer had applied an epoxy to try to hide the error rather than re-cut the entire top from a new piece. Some may think that it isn't too noticeable and may even feel embarrassed to go back to the store to have the problem rectified after all that has happened. Well, they shouldn't feel that way. I paid for a product and just because it was on sale doesn't mean I had to accept inferior or defective merchandise.

If you are in this situation call the store and register your complaint. They will immediately have the subcontractor send someone out to look at the defect. One of two things will happen and you can decide which is best for you. Within a few days, you should receive a call from either the subcontractor or the store offering a reasonable credit (say, twenty to twenty-five percent) to keep the item, or for a total remake. At first, the store called me and offered a five percent discount to keep the product. I responded that five percent wasn't worth it to me since the original cost with installation was around six thousand dollars. I told them to remake the counter and let me know when it would be available for total installation. I also reinforced the fact that I expected a plumber to be present to reconnect the faucet and drain the same day of the granite installation.

The time and labor, along with the materials to remake the counters, cost much more than the $300 credit the company was offering me, and I knew it. End of conversation.

Well, not actually. Two days later, I received a call from the corporate headquarters of the home goods store indicating that they read the entire report about the new problem, the plumbing error and all the hassles I had to endure over the last month. They offered me a resolution of their own: Keep the original counter since the chip was in the back corner, where it wasn't too noticeable, and receive a twenty-five percent credit for the job or, if I insisted, they would replace the entire counter plus give me a $100 store credit for my trouble. Now the credit was up to $1,500 so it was an easy choice. I kept the original granite and took the $1,500 on my credit card.

As you can see, it was worth standing up for my consumer rights and I decided not to let a large company walk all over me. It wasn't a case of getting something for nothing; it was about getting what I was promised when I contracted with them. I did not need an attorney as long as I was able to take the time and stand up for myself.

Case Four: Dishwasher

This is another situation dealing with the larger home goods stores. The policy is simple: Buy from us and let us install; we will guarantee our workmanship almost forever. It sounded good so I purchased my new dishwasher from the store and paid a flat labor installation cost up front. Wow, that was simple and it would make my life so easy.

The installation worked out well and the new unit was ready in less than an hour. I was totally pleased and thought this was the end...until the dishwasher came loose about a week later and fell forward from its position under the kitchen counter. I immediately called the store to report the problem; customer service took the complaint and indicated that someone from that department would call me back shortly. (Remember to pin them down as to what "shortly" means: in a few hours, days or somewhere within your lifetime.)

I realized the customer service department was talking about "in my lifetime" when I still hadn't received any follow-up a week later. I called customer service back and gave them my phone number so the representative could see the record and let me know what was going on. It turns out that the customer service department had no record of my call from a week earlier, even though I gave them the name of the person I spoke with. Again I was informed that the department would get back to me—and this time I pinned them down for a specific time.

Another seventy-two hours passed and nothing. In my game, it's not three strikes and you're out; I only allow two. Now was the time to go into action and use the aggressive approach. If I didn't go on the offensive by making myself forceful, these large companies with their massive, complicated systems would leave me stranded in no-man's-land forever.

This time I showed up in the store and insisted on seeing a manager. They sent over the manager of the day, which is like sending a boy to do a man's job. I explained my situation and he proceeded to say that he would look into the problem and get back to me. I didn't agree to go home and wait. Instead, I took the aggressive approach, which was to inform the MOD that I was not leaving until the problem was rectified to my satisfaction. The MOD just looked at me (remember, the next person who speaks loses!) and, after we finished our staring little contest, he finally agreed to get the division manager immediately. The problem was solved, but it took some doing on my part by showing up in the store so they couldn't blow off my phone call.

An installer came to redo the installation. Happy ending? Not quite. Two weeks later, the dishwasher fell out from under the counter again. But this time I had a direct contact to the division manager. I called and reported the problem in depth and, naturally, the manager apologized and said he would send the installer out again. At this point I could either agree or take a different approach. Remember, I use the two strikes and you're out theory, so I told the manager that I felt the installer was incompetent and I did not want that same person in my house again. I also stated that my time was worth more than his labor. Each time I left my office early to meet with the installer cost me far more than this whole job was worth.

Now is the time to take the lead and tell the manager what you want and expect. I suggested he send someone to pick up the dishwasher and give me a refund, and I would purchase the unit elsewhere, even if it cost me a little more. In the long run, I would be saving a lot by not having to keep leaving my office to meet with the installers that this store sent. Knowing the store really didn't want the used unit back and feeling they had had ample opportunity to perform in a businesslike manner, I put the manager in a position to say, "What can we do to keep you happy and keep you as a customer?" Those were the magical words I was waiting to hear.

I said I'd keep the unit if I could bring in my own installer to do the work properly and if the store would pay for that installation. He agreed, refunded my cost for the store installation and paid for a professional to properly install the dishwasher. This would have never happened had the store given me the proper courtesy from the onset instead of spinning me around in circles.

Like most consumers, all I expect is the service promised without making me feel like the store is doing me a favor. All anyone could want is respect, courtesy, an upheld promise and a quick response to any problem that may arise. Isn't that what customer service is all about?

Case Five: Front Door

Here is a problem dealing with a large national home goods lumber company. I ordered a new front door with sidelights, manufactured by one of those well-known door and window manufacturers. The door was priced just right and for only around $550, the store would remove the old door, install the new one and guarantee the work.

In order to have the installer come out and assess the

job, I was required to pay thirty-five dollars. If I accepted the terms of the installation, that money would be applied to the entire job. On the other hand, if I refused the installation, I lost the thirty-five dollars.

I gave the store my credit card, ordered the door and asked the installer to check out the job.

Wow, did I have my eyes opened when the installer got through with me! The $550 for installation ended up costing over $1,200. He stated that this was not a "normal installation" (sound familiar?). After measuring the job, he realized that the height of the new door and sidelights was slightly less than the doorway by one and a half inches. This wasn't really a big deal; it would have been much worse if it were the other way around and the door were too large, requiring the entire frame to be rebuilt.

It was explained to me that to install this door, two pieces of filler wood would have to be placed on top to fill the void, which would make the job more expensive. Since I happen to know a lot about construction, let me explain that it doesn't have to cost much more. We are talking about two boards of what is called one-by-four, cut to seventy-two inches in length. Once these are nailed into place, the opening is shortened to accept the new door. It would take any master carpenter ten minutes at most to cut these boards and install them properly—not a case of rocket science and definitely not worth an additional $650.

These subcontractors must not only make money for themselves but also give a percentage to the store. This is up selling and the average person has no idea that they are being taken for a ride, so they simply pay the bill.

Here is where I had to be my own advocate. I let the installer leave then go back to the store and get the MOD. I explained what happened and that I did not like being duped into thinking that the store was sending out a qualified carpenter who would be giving me a fair evaluation, when it obviously wasn't. Out of principle, I received my thirty-five dollars back and a ten percent discount for my trouble, and decided to hire my own carpenter. The end result was that the entire job, including painting both sides of the door, came to around $750.

No, we are still not done. There was a manufacturing problem with the door: the frame was not quite square. Also, the steel door was slightly bent in one corner. My carpenter called the store and ordered an entirely new door to replace the bad one. How did it end up? The store never placed the order, even though they were called twice over the next few weeks.

That's when I went into full gear. I went back to the store and talked with one of the managers, who found the record of the order but saw that nothing had been done about it. (Remember what I said earlier: Know what you want before you go back to the store.) He asked if the door could be repaired and repainted afterward. My carpenter indicated that he could pound out the bend, sand it smooth and repaint the door for about one hundred dollars…so what do you think I asked for? I requested a fifteen percent discount and received ten percent, which was around $420, based on the cost of the door.

Don't be shy. If a large or small company can get away with something, they will try. You as the consumer may often feel helpless and unsure of how to handle the situation—but as you can see from these various cases, you should not think there is nothing you can do. You can always pursue the issue. Most companies will create an arrangement to settle the matter to your satisfaction—but you must be persistent.

Over the years, many large chain stores have gone broke. Most of the time, it wasn't directly because of poor management policies—but it is all related to how the stores treat customers and the type of service they offer (just look at stores like Grant, E. J. Korvettes and Bradley's, which had longevity in the seventies). Lately, some major stores started out with great customer service but as they grew and tried to increase profitability, something had to give. And customer service is always the first thing to go. The thinking is that they already have people trained to come to their store, so why offer good customer service anymore?

This is why many good restaurants fail and I also believe it is one of the reasons the airline industry has been in trouble for so many years, even before 9/11. Just look at Southwest Airlines, which has been profitable since its formation in the early seventies. It isn't just low fares, but the way in which they handle their customers. To them, the customer is the most important part of their business; without us, there would be no airline.

There is an old term, "pot lash," which means to give more than is expected. Consider any well-run business that offers great service and gives the customer more than expected, and you will find a long-standing, successful business.

Chapter 5

Municipal Nightmares

Home repairs and home goods stores are bad enough, but dealing with your local government is one of my favorite issues. You pay your local taxes and expect some consideration for the money you invest into the system. But things don't always work out the way you want them to.

What do you do when your local government has multiple services in place but the employees of the city government try not to follow policy and write their own systems? You must fight to make these workers do their jobs and be accountable for their actions, no matter how lazy and complacent they are.

Case One: Trash Removal

I moved into a quiet neighborhood over twenty years ago. One of the first things I received was a welcome packet from the city with information about some of the services and city rules for everyone to follow. One rule that stuck in my mind was that on weekdays, work in the neighborhood could not start before 7 a.m. (on weekends, the start time was 9 a.m.). I was impressed that this was backed by a city ordinance.

Every worker followed the rules except the trash removal people. During the winter, the removal, which occurred twice a week, went according to the rules. But during my first summer there, garbage trucks with their horns and grinders were there at 5:45 a.m., waking up everyone in the neighborhood.

I called the trash department to explain the problem and was told that since it was getting very hot by midmorning, the workers wanted to start early to avoid the heat. My response was that I appreciated their plight, but that it wasn't my problem and I shouldn't have to suffer for it. I was entitled to the quiet sanctity of my home according to city code and explained that all other work in the neighborhood was restricted until after 7 a.m.

Later that day, I received a call from the head of the public works department trying to convince me that not only was it hot, but the city didn't have to comply with its own ordinance. I listened politely then responded that the city was also restricted and I'd make an issue of it if it persisted.

The next week came and the same thing happened right around 5:45 a.m. Again I called the public works department and gave them a polite ultimatum. They said they understood and I decided to wait until the third week to see if the problem occurred again. At around 6:10 a.m., the trash trucks were out in full force. This time, I spoke directly with the mayor's office, sternly informing them that I was prepared to take legal action and ask the court to issue an injunction. I also wrote a detailed letter to the mayor outlining the problem (and sent a copy to the public works manager). It was amazing how things quieted down for the rest of that summer.

The winter passed and we entered the next summer, when the problem surfaced again. I went directly to the mayor and city council and, about two weeks after the meeting, received a letter from the council informing me that the city was exempt from the ordinance. I could understand the exemption for emergency services but not for routine services.

To take things further, I called the police and requested an officer be in the neighborhood the next time trash was due for pick up. The chief of police called me and asked if he could settle the matter. I said that it was the function of the police department to enforce the city ordinances no matter who was involved. He tried to tell me he couldn't do anything and I told him that if he couldn't, then I would.

The next morning I went to my local court and asked the clerk how to file an injunction against someone to cease and desist doing an action. He was very helpful and walked me through the process, though I didn't tell him that it was the city I was placing the injunction against.

I filed the injunction and got it signed by a judge, which now meant that the city had to adhere to its own ordinances. This would also force the police to take action. The next time the trash collectors showed up before 7 a.m., I called the police and made it clear that I had an injunction, and they responded by kicking the trash collectors out of the neighborhood until the appropriate time.

This brought a personal phone call from the mayor himself, who was now ready to work out some sort of resolution. The answer was that the garbage company would not enter my neighborhood again before 7 a.m. In fact, that lasted for seventeen years until one morning the recycling truck, which is a subcontractor, showed up before that time. All it took was one phone call on my part and it has never happened again.

Sometimes, to stand up for your rights, you may actually have to fight city hall. If you were a landscaper, carpenter, etc. who started work in the neighborhood before 7 a.m., rest assured that the police would have stopped you. But what goes for the little guys also goes for the big guys, if you know how to stand up to them.

Case Two: Special Pickup

My city considers paint cans, even from latex paint, a form of hazardous material based on an age-old regulation when paint was mostly oil-based.

I needed to get rid of twenty cans of old paint but was told I must solidify them using kitty litter then put them out on the curb with the lids off on a day for special pickups. I followed the instructions, called when they were ready for retrieval and put them at the curb. The day went by and at around 4 p.m., they were still there so I called about the pickup. I was told they would be picked up the very next day, so I left them out all night.

The next day came and went, as did the next day, and the next, and so on. Each day I called the city and received a different excuse. Finally I was told they would be taken the next week on the regularly scheduled special pickup day. Again the day came and went so I called the head of public works, who assured me it would happen soon. Nothing did for another seven days—my paint cans were still sitting on the curb.

Want to know how I solved the problem? It was a no-brainer. I took eight of the cans, placed them in two boxes, walked into the mayor's office and put them on his assistant's desk, telling her I was making it the mayor's problem. I also informed her that I would bring the rest over in a few days.

Of course, she said I couldn't leave them there, but my response was that the mayor was supposed to run the city and if his staff of workers did not do their jobs, then the buck stopped there, in his office. What he did with the cans was strictly up to him. With that, I walked out, leaving my name and address along with the kitty littered paint cans.

It worked very well. The next day I received a call from the public works director, who had been personally instructed to come to my house to pick up the rest of the cans. He did just that and apologized. I told him he needed to do his job better and make sure that the people who worked under his direction were also doing their jobs.

Case Three: Snow Removal

I live at the end of a cul-de-sac so, regarding snow removal, either the city does not shovel my circle or ends up dumping the snow right in front of my driveway just after I finished shoveling it.

When I first moved into the neighborhood and we had a horrendous winter, the city kept doing just that. They dropped large mounds of ice in front of my driveway apron, so it was impossible to move them or get my car out when I needed to. I called the city snow removal line late one night only to find it was always busy. I guess they took it off the hook so they didn't have to bother with anyone calling.

After being trapped in my house after trying to remove the snow for a solid hour, I had an idea. I called the next number in the sequence, hoping it was the actual ring-down number and it was. This immediately got me through to the dispatcher, who had no choice but to talk to me. He understood my problem and sent the truck back within minutes to clear a path. I guess he figured that if I could get to him, it was the least he could do for me. You see, I had to try all sorts of tricks to get the city workers, who were being paid by me indirectly, to do their jobs. Government workers become so complacent and often do their work not per city regulations, but according to how they determine it should be.

From that point on, I had the dispatcher's number and would use it to my advantage. Then one day, the city changed the phone system and now no one could get through except on the direct number. Well, that wouldn't do. So the day after the first snowfall, I went directly over to the snow removal office and personally met with the head of operations. We had a long discussion and I got him to give me the private number again. Wanting to ensure my success going forward, I sent him a holiday gift with my thanks.

Did it work? Naturally! I never had a pile in front of my driveway again.

This past year, however, my dispatcher friend retired and the city replaced him. I was away when the first big storm materialized—and the truck not only pushed the snow in front of my driveway but its blade broke my storm drain and the concrete, and destroyed the first four feet of my lawn. I found the mess when I returned so I called public works and reported the problem. I identified the damage as a hazard to the children in the neighborhood, which got their attention. They placed a restricted area around the sewer housing until spring.

As spring approached and nothing was done to repair the problem, I called the mayor's office and spoke with the coordinator. When she heard what happened, it took two weeks for action—and an apology. The sewer was rebuilt, and the sidewalk and my lawn replaced.

This just shows that you must be assertive and move from office to office if necessary until something happens. Each office will attempt to pass the buck to another division, which is why I went to the mayor directly. Keep moving up the chain of command until you command someone's attention!

Case Four: Leaf Removal

In the fall, our city refuse department performs leaf removal duty. This year, various contracted lawn services in the neighborhood removed and piled up so many leaves that it blocked the street entirely. I called the refuse department about this and they referred me to the city code department. The code department refused to do anything so they sent me to the police, who would come and check out the situation and report back to the city. What a waste of police manpower!

Not satisfied with the outcome and realizing that there were better jobs for the police to do, I wrote a letter to the mayor and city council. They were appalled at the way it was handled and agreed that it wasted the time of the police department. The city manager was brought into the picture and it trickled down to public works. Nobody was fired, but I assure you that when someone calls in the future, they will jump to do their jobs instead of passing the buck from one department to the next.

Case Five: Street Safety

On one of our major streets in the city, two lanes turn left, but the dotted line separating the lanes has been gone for years. In most cases, one of the two drivers turning left tends to swerve into the lane of the other driver, causing a fender bender or a near-miss. I personally have had eight near-misses.

I went to the department of streets and requested that the lines be repainted, which the person in charge assured me would happen by the next year. I assume that answer was supposed to satisfy me, but I asked if he was out of his mind! The problem had already existed for years and should have been fixed immediately. He told me he couldn't do anything, so I told him that I would see about that!

I wrote a very sarcastic and scathing letter to the mayor and council, including a point about the lack of action taken by the department of streets and the safety issue it involved. I raised the question that maybe it would take an accidental death for the city to respond, and this got their attention. I also let the mayor know that I was sending a copy of the letter to the local news paper and even offered the city $100 for the paint if they could get one of their workers to redo the lines on the street.

Three days later I got a letter signed by the mayor and all of the council indicating that there was no need for me to give them $100. They sent an inspector out to look at the situation and forty-eight hours later, the lines were painted as they should have been years ago. A simple solution to a big problem sometimes only requires that the right words get through to the right people.

Chapter 6

Insurance Issues

What a fantastic idea to be able to purchase a travel insurance plan to protect the cost of those expensive cruises or trips abroad! Actually, they sound great up front but just try to use it. It isn't easy.

Case One: Travel Insurance

The inevitable finally happened; I had to cancel a cruise because of some unexpected surgery. Of course, I had my insurance coverage so there wouldn't be any problem in getting the cost of the cruise back. Or so I thought.

I called the insurance company and said that I had to cancel and wanted to exercise my option to use my insurance plan to be reimbursed for the cost of the cruise. The customer service representative issued a claim number and sent me a claim form to complete, which I did.

After filing the form, I waited and waited. It took a couple of telephone calls and I was told, as most good insurance companies tell their customers, that it was "in process." Being experienced in dealing with companies, I asked what "in process" meant. Each time I was told something different. After my fourth call, I told the customer service person to note on my record that if I did not hear something in the next seven working days, I would pursue this matter legally. (I had already given them my medical forms, signed by my surgeon and notarized.)

Finally, after seven days, not including the six long weeks before that, I received one of those lengthy letters explaining why they would not cover my claim. The insurance company tried to justify its position by stressing that my medical condition was pre-existing. The surgery was sudden, so I have no idea where they came up with that idea!

Well, I wasn't going to stand for this. I called and wrote them a letter indicating that when I booked the cruise and paid for the insurance, I did not have any knowledge of the condition requiring surgery, despite what they had determined after reviewing my charts. My position was based on the company's statement that if I had purchased the insurance within three days of paying the initial deposit for the cruise, pre-existing conditions would have been waived.

The return letter I received indicated that this was not the proper interpretation of the statement and that I still wasn't covered. Again, I responded that there was no pre-existing condition, and that I did not have a "pre-existing condition clause" in my policy since it was supposed to have been waived. We were at an impasse over the interpretation of the English language!

I was in Maryland and the insurance company was in California, so I guess they figured I would not do anything because of the distance and the cost to sue. Wrong again! I had to learn to use the system to my best advantage.

The first thing I did was contact the California Insurance Department. After being led around for a few hours, I finally reached someone who knew about the system and agreed to send me a complaint form. When it arrived, I not only had to fill it out in detail but I had to submit all letters and documentation to verify my complaint. I did exactly as requested. About three weeks went by and I received a letter with all of my original documentation in tact. The letter stated that even though they felt I was correct, this issue really fell under the insurance commission of my state, Maryland. This was a plus since it meant the California company would have to come to Maryland to argue the case.

I called and received a claim form from the Maryland Insurance Commission, which I filed with a copy of all my papers, as well as a copy of the California Insurance Commission's letter. I also called the Department of Corporations in California and, with their help, found out who the resident agent was for the insurance company. Then I got the appropriate forms to file with my state court. I had two choices: file only with the insurance commission or file with the court system in Maryland. I chose to do both since I knew that the insurance company would be served by the state insurance commission *and* by the court to appear in Maryland.

At this point, I put the insurance company on notice, telling them that I filed with the insurance commission in my state and with the court for restitution. This was to let them know that I meant business—and that I found out that their selling insurance to a Maryland resident actually gave me the right to file in a Maryland court.

The insurance company was in the process of answering the Maryland Insurance Commissioner's request when I sent a notice to appear in court (through certified mail) to the resident agent in California. That did the trick. I received a call from the president of the insurance company, though I didn't answer until he left three messages over a ten-day period. I had decided to treat them just like they had treated me when I first sent in my claim!

Finally, I called him back. The first thing he tried was to go over the language again to justify why they weren't paying. My response was that the language was quite clear and their interpretation was a way to get out of paying claims—and that I would leave it up to the insurance commission and the courts. I did tell him that if I were found wrong, I would go by whatever the judge determined was correct. He seemed to get the picture that I intended to take this all the way.

I explained that he would either have to come to court in Maryland or send an attorney, which would be very costly, but that I would be happy to go to court since it was close by and I was almost retired with plenty of time on my hands. What I didn't tell him was that if he came to Maryland or sent an attorney, I would ask the judge for a continuance at the eleventh hour so it would cost them big bucks to answer my complaint a second time.

In Maryland, if I received judgment, I could garnish their account or the insurance commission would suspend their ability to do business in Maryland until my claim was paid. Basically, I sort of had them over a barrel and it would cost them more to fight the claim than make a payment.

Well, you guessed it. Two days later I received a call that I would receive a check for the cost of the cruise. I was quite happy to eat the fifteen dollars it cost me to file in the courts.

The check came in but since they ran me around awhile, I decided to still pursue the claim with the insurance commission. My point was that if this company did this to me, imagine how many others they had done it to, and that it was not in the state's best interest to allow them to continue to write insurance in Maryland.

This situation went up for a lengthy review with the state but nothing was ever done about it. Even though most state agencies are there for consumer protection, don't be fooled. These same agencies are actually also protecting business interests—because businesses have more money and often pay more taxes than individual consumers do.

Case Two: Automobile Insurance

We all rely on our automobile insurance for coverage, so we pay our premiums in hopes that it will protect us when we need it. In most cases the companies stand by their products and handle their claims quickly and efficiently. But not always.

One day after visiting one of those large box hardware stores, I found a dent in my car's front door. I had noticed some children riding around on one of the larger push-carts normally used for lumber, so I went back in the store and spoke with the manager, who told me to go through my own insurance.

I called my insurance company and reported the incident, thinking it would be covered under the comprehensive part of my policy. This meant my $100 deductible would apply. The insurance company had a different idea and wanted to place this under the accident portion of my policy, so my $500 deductible would apply. We spent quite a few weeks going back and forth over the terms of the policy. They told me I didn't qualify under the comprehensive portion due to exclusions and that I did not fall into one of the ten approved categories. I told them that this should come under "mischievous behavior" since I saw the children playing with the large carts as I entered the store. Mischievous behavior falls under comprehensive coverage and is not considered an actual accident.

After a few months, I refused to accept what the insurance company had determined. I felt that under the terms of the policy, I was correct and would prevail. I would not accept their check and fixed the door myself after taking a series of photos. Keep in mind that big insurance companies think it's easy to take advantage of the little guy. They have deep pockets and a full-time legal staff; therefore, I had to take action into my own hands and utilize the government resources already in place.

I filed with the state insurance commission, which opened an investigation that took six weeks. After that time, I received a letter from the state investigator saying he received information from the insurance company that the incident wasn't covered, so he accepted this as truth. Some state employees work but don't really do their jobs—there is a huge difference! They are going to get paid even if they really don't accomplish anything. This investigator should have read the information and brought it to a higher level rather than just sweeping it under the carpet.

I wrote a reply to the investigator and sent a copy to the insurance commissioner directly, which did achieve my point. The claim was assigned to another investigator and I was immediately given a date for arbitration.

Months went by and as we got closer to that date, I received a call from one of the attorneys representing the insurance company. She informed me that three of them would be at the hearing and wanted to know the name of my attorney so she could talk with him directly. I explained that I did not need an attorney and was acting on my own behalf. She was stunned.

About a day before the hearing, another attorney for the insurance company called to offer me a settlement: the cost of the repair less my $100 deductible. I refused, stating that it was not good enough, and told her what I wanted: the full cost of the repair and my record in CLUE (Comprehensive Loss Underwriting Exchange) expunged. She said she'd call me back. (CLUE is a system wherein insurance companies report fender benders or home-owner's losses. This allows all insurance companies to track your loss record, which helps determine your ability to get insurance should you decide to change companies.) About an hour later, she did call back. They would give me full repair value but would not remove my CLUE report or change this claim to a comprehensive loss. Therefore, I refused the deal again and told her I would leave it up to the insurance commissioner and the arbitrators.

The next day came and we were to meet at the office of the insurance commissioner for the arbitration hearing. It was late fall and some snow was falling but not enough to stop the hearing. I had to travel forty-five minutes and they had a two-and-a-half-hour-drive late in the afternoon on the Wednesday before Thanksgiving. I am describing this to set the stage for what I did next.

About three hours before the hearing, I received a call from one of the attorneys making sure that I was not going to settle. I refused to unless it was on my terms since they ran me around for months over the $630 claim. I looked at the weather and, about thirty minutes before the hearing, called the insurance commissioner's arbitration team to ask if I could withdraw my claim or extend the date. I was told I could do either, so I asked to extend the case to another date. Everyone agreed, except the three attorneys for the insurance company, who hadn't arrived yet. We were rescheduled for the week between Christmas and New Year's Day. My guess is that, when they did finally arrive, I really ticked them off—but that is exactly what the insurance company did to me!

As the new date came closer, I again received a call trying to settle the claim but refused, saying I wanted to keep the date. So the arbitration was set on December 29 at around 2 p.m. This time I waited until five minutes before it began to call and request a withdrawal of the claim altogether. The young lady from the insurance commissioner's office said she would close the case and notify everyone, including the three attorneys, to go home.

You are probably asking yourself why I did this twice. Once I found out that the insurance company was sending three killer attorneys to take on little old me, I knew what I had to do. I realized that two days of paying attorneys and expenses for the trip probably cost the insurance company in excess of $5,000 to defend against me. This was all the satisfaction I needed. I was willing to forgo the $630 just to see the insurance company lose the money. (For the record, I had already changed to another insurance company months before.)

Don't be afraid to take on the big businesses. Use your head and the resources available—and in most cases you will get some form of satisfaction. This time, my satisfaction was seeing them spend loads of money to defend against one person with a dented door. What holiday joy!

Case Three: Auto Glass Repair

Here is a simple situation where, again, as a consumer, I had to stand up for myself to be successful in the end. A stone cracked my front windshield. I called the insurance company and it was decided that the crack was large enough to replace the glass, which I did. Wouldn't you know it? About a week after the new glass was installed, a truck kicked up a stone and again I had a small chip.

I called the insurance company and none of us could figure the odds of that happening twice in such a short period of time. This time, I elected to accept the glass repair since it was not subject to my deductible and was guaranteed for the life of my car.

The repair was finished and seemed sort of invisible. I drove with it for almost a year when I started to notice a small fracture line appearing. I immediately called my insurance company and requested the glass be changed, and they agreed. But remember the "guaranteed for life" part? All of a sudden that disappeared! When I spoke with the glass company that gave the guarantee, they said the new repair would now be subject to my deductible.

I immediately called the insurance company back and asked what the guarantee meant now that, a year later, the "lifetime" part was no longer being honored. They said that if the repair failed, the company that did it would return the fee they received from the insurance company and the claim would start again from ground zero. My comment was, "That's good for the insurance company but where is *my* guarantee?" The customer service representative said that was simply how it was done.

I could not leave this alone. Something was wrong with this picture: I was offered a guarantee and when the repair failed, the guarantee was reversed. The way I saw it was that the glass company was paid sixty-five dollars to do the repair and they were the ones offering the guarantee. If the repair failed, they should be obligated to replace the glass and my deductible should not apply.

I am forceful, so I called the claims office of my insurance company and got the name of the person in charge. Then I wrote a letter to that person explaining the dilemma, along with how I perceived this so-called guarantee.

It seemed to work because the next thing I knew, I received a letter from a claims adjuster who informed me that I should replace the glass using any company I chose and the deductible would indeed be waived. Once again, the insurance company had promised something at first and then tried to walk out of the commitment. If they denied the same hundred dollars to ten thousand customers a year that they tried to deny to me, they would save $1,000,000 in deductibles that should have been waived in similar circumstances.

Let them walk all over you and they win every time.

Chapter 7

Getting What You Pay for From Air Travel

I remember when the airline industry was regulated and we consumers were treated like human beings rather than cattle on the way to the slaughter. The planes were comfortable and clean, and the food was more than palatable. Obviously, the airline industry changed in trying to reach better profit margins; now they tolerate us as passengers but treat us with the utmost disrespect.

I don't think this has anything to do with 9/11, but since the concept of travel by flying has increased markedly in the United States, the airlines no longer have to be courteous and concerned for the traveler. Sure, they provide customer service but it is really nothing more than some employees who are there to run interference (the one exception to all of this is Southwest Airlines, which has been—and still is—the most successful, customer-oriented airline for the past thirty-five years).

Case One: Switching Seats

A couple of years ago, I had to fly with one of the biggest and oldest carriers in the United States from the East to the West. My wife recently had back surgery and could not sit rigid for five hours in those so-called "seats" and I wasn't sure what to do other than purchasing a first-class ticket. When I inquired about the cost, I commented to the reservationist that I didn't have time to mortgage my house to pay for the two tickets, so I had to go back to the drawing board.

A friend of mine gave me a great idea so I called and booked three seats in one row. This would allow me to afford the flight and I could lift the center armrests, which meant my wife could change her position easily. Of course, the airlines have such restrictive standards that they made it almost impossible to buy the three seats. The only way I could do it was to put one in her first name, the second in her middle name and one in my name. When she checked in, her driver's license would reflect her first, middle and last names.

I was willing to buy two seats using her first name,

but the airline said they would not check her in since she was only one person, although airlines can sell two seats to an obese person when it means more profits for them. I guess if my wife were overweight, it would have been to her advantage, but she isn't. Anyway, having two sets of standards is typical for the airline industry.

We were able to get all three seats reserved with a special notation on the reservation that the seats must be kept together for medical purposes. I thought this was great and there would be no problems...until we showed up for the flight. We went to check in and it turned out that the airline decided to randomly recycle the seats for their own benefit. We now had two seats on one side of the plane and one window seat on the other.

I approached the ticket counter with the problem and, even though they could see the notation on the reservation, they informed us that they could not do anything to upset the computer. What that really meant was it wasn't in their best interest to keep their promise to us, since I already paid my money and there was a no-refund policy. I'm sure they oversold the aircraft by the usual thirty percent, which complicated matters even more.

They told me to talk with the gate agent (which is called "passing the buck to someone else"). Instead, I requested a refund on the one odd seat, but was refused. If I didn't use the ticket, I would lose it. Again, the airline was adopting its usual attitude of "you need us more than we need you, so do it our way."

My wife and I got to the gate and spoke with the gate agent, who may have been one of the nastiest, most arrogant, and rudest people I have ever met. I guess she had an attitude because airline employees have a form of ownership in the airlines and therefore no longer have to worry about the quality of their work. They think they are infallible, or at least untouchable.

As a point, I never raised my voice and instead tried to use logic, but soon found out that logic wouldn't fly. The gate agent actually told me that the only obligation of the airline was to get me from point A to point B safely, and she could do nothing else.

So, I resorted to an old trick: call for reservations using my cell phone to see if any seats were still open so I could get them to change our seats over the phone. This was totally unnecessary, but I had to figure out a way to beat their stupid system. The reservationist told me that within forty-five minutes of boarding, the computer was locked and the change could only be done at the airport; at the same time, the airport workers were telling me that they did not have the authority to make any changes. It was a catch-22.

I got to the point of practically begging, and finally the reservationist told me to go to the special services counter of the airline for help. Isn't it pathetic that I paid for three seats due to a medical problem yet I was reduced to running all over the airport for help? I could have gone home but would have lost the cost of the three seats as well as my hotel deposits. The airlines really had us over a barrel—but, actually, I don't blame the airlines as much as I blame our politicians for allowing the situation to get to this point.

I ran all the way to the other end of the terminal with only thirty minutes left before take off. When I got to the counter, the person in front of me was in no hurry, asking the special needs representative a million questions. When I finally got to the front of the line, I explained my problem in detail and quickly, mentioning the gate manager and her attitude. She immediately accessed the computer and moved the person in the window seat of our row to my lone seat on the other side of the plane, now giving us all three seats together. She also said that she was going to report the other employee.

So the problem was solved with twenty minutes to go, but it had all been totally unnecessary. The airlines and their policies are out of control. The government needs to take a stand and force them to change their attitudes and not only follow more stringent regulations, but also design universal passenger rights. We have all experienced or heard about lost luggage problems, delayed flights and passengers sitting captive on the runway for up to nine hours. Consumers should make it known to our representatives that they need to do more to help us, rather than always finding ways to put a band-aid on an increasingly worsening situation and protecting the rights of the airlines. Of course, it doesn't bother them because the airlines will do anything to give extended courtesy to senators or congresspersons.

Case Two: Unsanitary Conditions On-Board

I had always looked forward to flying first-class to Europe, and was at the stage in my life when I could book those seats. I was excited to know I would be comfortable in a newer jumbo jet with wide seats and some slightly pampering service. This would make the thirteen hours go by more quickly and in a more relaxed atmosphere.

When I arrived at the airport, I checked in and was told that with first-class tickets, I had the right to use the airlines' sky lounge. This was really nice since they had free food and drinks for us while we sat in comfort, waiting for the flight. In what seemed like no time, my wife and I were called to board.

I looked out the window and saw a Boeing 767, which, even though it is twenty years old, is still a really nice aircraft, or so I thought. We boarded and I got the shock of my life. This plane looked clean on the surface but a closer look showed it to be not only rundown but filthy. I didn't live like that in my home so why would this major U.S. carrier expect me to fly in filth?

I fortunately carry Lysol wipes so I was able to wipe the dirty seats and arm rests. As for the tray table I would be eating on, I had trouble getting the dirt and dried food off, which must have been there for the full age of the plane. At first people laughed, then they all starting asking me for wipes when they realized how filthy the plane was, especially considering the money they were spending.

We weren't ready to take off yet, so I went to use the bathroom only to find that two of the three first-class accommodations were out of service and had flooded during the inbound trip from Europe. The area and seats around the bathrooms actually stank. I asked the flight staff why they hadn't been fixed and was told it would have taken three to four hours. I looked at her perplexed since the flight had arrived at 11 a.m. and was now leaving at 6:45 p.m. She added that the problem had been reported upon landing but no one had done anything— and now we had to leave.

We departed on time but having one bathroom presented a problem since we had to use the ones in economy class, which always had a line. We got to Italy, filth and all, but one of our friends, who had been traveling with us, started to get sick. She had eaten the fish on the plane; when we talked with others as we went through customs, it turned out that all of those who ate the fish were also starting to feel sick. Our friend spent the next twenty-four hours vomiting and, by all indications, it appeared that the fish may have been contaminated. Who knows how the food was prepared or how long it sat without refrigeration before it was loaded onto the plane?

Personally, I could not rest without letting the airline and the F.A.A. know about the situation, especially since there are regulations pertaining even to the sanitary conditions of the aircraft. I wrote a lengthy letter to the airlines' customer service department and sent a copy of the complaint to the F.A.A. It only took two months for the airline to send me one of their standard letters of apology, which included a coupon for two free tickets to anywhere in the United States.

Well, that was nice, but did it get their attention enough to make sure that their planes were clean in the future? I doubt it. I will take odds that when I fly to Europe again and if I have to use one of their planes, it will most likely be as dirty as the last one.

If the airlines are cutting costs by not cleaning their planes, I would be happy if they would give each and every one of us passengers a rag with which to clean our space. No wonder we have sick people coming into the country. Some are sick when they board the plane and others probably get sick after flying on one of these unsanitary crafts. Look at all the problems the cruise industry has had with illnesses onboard, so I won't be surprised when the same thing inevitably happens on airplanes.

We must all demand more and quit settling for mediocrity. The more people who take the time to complain, the more attention the airlines may give to the seriousness of these problems. If they can't find the time to fix a bathroom, I can only imagine what they will not fix when it comes to the mechanics of the plane itself.

Case Three: True Customer Service

Dealing with one of the most successful U.S. carriers is indeed a pleasure. I had a ticket for a flight last year but needed to cancel because of illness. This carrier does not do refunds, but does make it extremely easy for passengers to reuse their tickets at a future date without having penalties that are more than the ticket itself.

In this case, when I requested the cancellation, instead of banking the money in my account with the airline, I was issued a cash voucher for the full amount of the ticket, which was good for six months toward a future flight with that airline. After four months, I realized I wasn't going to use the voucher and called their help desk. I was told that during the last week, I could simply call again and the company would extend the voucher for another six months. I thought that was really good treatment since no other carrier would do that…and maybe that was the reason for their success. It is called common courtesy and good customer service, in the truest sense.

I waited a few weeks then did as I was instructed, only to be told that they did not issue extensions and the ticket value was a loss. I was angry and hurt that the airline I had trusted all these years was starting to become just like all the others.

I decided to write a letter to customer service, appealing to their good nature and explaining about what I had originally been told and what had finally transpired. I first received a card letting me know that my letter was being looked into (which was really unusual since no other airline I have ever communicated with acknowledged receiving my letters; the only way I had ever found out was by their response in eight to twelve weeks).

It only took two weeks for me to receive not a letter, but a personal call from a customer service specialist asking me to return her call directly, which I did. I was flabbergasted when she told me that they did have a policy change midstream and what I had originally been told was the old policy, but that she was going to extend the voucher for one year from the date of our telephone conversation this time only, in light of the change.

No other airline in the past fifteen years seemed to

consider me as a person and offer me such a high level of customer service. Most airlines today look for any way to keep your money and simply treat you like a number, not an individual.

The moral of this story is that it sometimes doesn't hurt to write a polite letter rather than throw your hands up in the air. Who knows? Maybe some of those bigger airlines may get the message that there is more to being successful than just the bottom line.

Chapter 8

How to Handle Homeowners' Repairs

We all pay for insurance with the hopes of never having to use it. For all of the homeowners with coverage in case of fire, flood, theft or other massive damage, only a small, unfortunate few ever need to place a claim. That's how insurance companies make their money—by playing the odds. However, if you ever do need reimbursement, make sure you get everything you are entitled to. That is the only reason you've been paying into the insurance system for all these years.

One night, I woke up at around 2 a.m. to a hissing sound from downstairs. When I crept into my kitchen, I slid across the floor in a puddle of water. So it wasn't a snake! A pipe had obviously ruptured.

That's when the fun began. Like most homeowners, I had insurance to cover this type of situation so I contacted the insurance company the next day to determine how to handle the loss. They sent over a professional whose job was to clean up the immediate mess and place fans in my property to dry out the moisture and reduce the possibility of excessive mold growth.

This helped…until the adjuster from my insurance company arrived two days later. This person seemed helpful, courteous and concerned, but he was not really working for me—he was working for the insurance company. The adjuster's job was to improve the situation at the least possible cost to the insurance company while trying to keep me, the insured, happy and quiet.

After about two hours on my property, he said he'd have to go back to the office to work up an estimate of the repairs and that this process would take a few days, which it did. I was also told that if I used one of their recommended contractors, the insurance company would guarantee the work.

Finally, after three days, I received the phone call from the adjuster. Based upon the average repair and construction costs in my area, he determined the damage to be around $20,000 (this is not the actual number), and offered to write me a check in that amount, less my $500 deductible, along with a statement releasing the insurance company from any further liability.

I decided that before I accepted the payment and signed off on the claim, I'd like one of their recommended contractors to come in and bid on the job. This was arranged—but the estimate for repairs was given to that contractor before he showed up at my house.

Don't be lulled into a false sense of security that your insurance has you covered. What usually happens is that the insurance company, in an attempt to save money, hires contractors who often slap the job together and move on to something else.

In this instance, one kitchen cabinet was damaged by water and the floor tile was coming up. My basement walls were also severely damaged, and some wallboard and electrical wires had to be replaced. Fortunately, I have some experience in repair work, which the average homeowner may not. Most accept the insurance company's preferred contractors, and in some cases this turns out to be a fantastic choice, but all too often the repairs end up being inferior and require you to hire another contractor to finish the job to your satisfaction. Even if the insurance guarantees the work, the mess and inconvenience of repair isn't worth having to do it twice.

The company's suggested contractor showed up and reviewed the estimate, as well as looking at the nature of the job. After about an hour in my house, he put a contract in front of me to sign, stating that it could be another $4,500 above the estimate. Rest assured that if I had signed the contract, it would have definitely been another $4,500 out of my pocket!

Before signing anything or accepting a check, I decided to call in a couple of contractors of my own to get a better feel of what had to be done and at what cost. Was I ever right in doing this! Both contractors showed me some things the insurance company missed in their determination of repairs. For example, they explained that replacing a single fifteen-year-old kitchen cabinet was almost impossible since they were all custom-made.

The insurance was just going to replace the tile but the sub-floor also had to be removed and replaced. The wallpaper in my kitchen had to be replaced, but the insurance never provided for the fact that the blinds were covered with the same wallpaper so they, too, would have to be replaced.

Understand that the insurance company expects their contractors to fix everything for their estimated price— and I am sure that everything would have been fixed using the insurance company's contractor…but *how* it would have been fixed is another story.

My two private contractors worked up a full, finished bid involving all new kitchen cabinets, replacing the sub-flooring and completing the entire job as I would have expected it to be done. I did not want a band-aid placed on the cut when surgery was required.

Those bids came in at $42,000 and $39,500, as opposed to the one from the insurance-appointed professional, who figured $19,000. When the insurance estimator came to my house, I presented her with my two estimates. Don't forget that you, the insured, have the right to use anyone you choose and do not have to accept the insurance company's contractors.

The insurance adjuster tried to convince me that she was not authorized to increase the payout to $40,000. When I asked her who could authorize it, she said the original $20,000 was all they would pay. This is why I had to know my rights! I was not obligated to accept what they wanted to hand me—I was entitled to full replacement value approximating the quality of what was there before the incident.

If you are ever in this situation, send the insurance company a letter stating your problem and demanding to receive the fair value of the repair, according to the terms of your policy. Make sure you send a copy to your state insurance commissioner, your agent and your attorney. Send everything by certified mail with a return receipt. Let them know that the longer you cannot use your house, the more you will expect to be compensated for your loss of use.

It worked like a charm for me! About five days later, I received a call from the adjuster that the company would authorize my repairs, which now included a new floor, all new kitchen cabinets, new wallpaper, blinds, carpet and a total rebuilding of the basement. The adjuster reserved the right to come in at different stages of the process to verify the repairs before giving the contractor more money.

However, one of the points that the adjuster made over and over again was that under the terms of the policy, the company was not responsible for the actual plumbing problem that caused the damage. I would have to pay for that repair myself.

The end result was that the insurance company paid $41,500 for the repairs and I paid sixty-seven cents for the section of pipe that broke, which was not covered in my policy!

Chapter 9

Don't Get Taken in by General Contractors

General contractors are the most upfront, forthright businesspeople any of us has ever had the pleasure of dealing with, right? Receiving a firm bid in writing means we can all rest easy: the job will be finished on schedule and exactly on budget. Yeah, sure! If you ever come across such a contractor, please let me know because I'd love to shake his hand!

We all dread the day when we have to call in a contractor for a building project. Those stories you hear are true, and sometimes it's simpler to just move than even consider doing a renovation. But since that isn't really a realistic approach, you have to do the renovations despite all of the potential problems.

First, you need to call in at least five different contractors for every job. "Why?" you may wonder. Because you will be lucky if three show up to their appointments, and out of those three, generally only two will come back with a bid price.

It is always advisable to make some form of sketch or list of what it is you want accomplished, otherwise each contractor will come up with something totally different. Of course, every now and then, you could run across that one contractor who is also a great designer and makes a layout of exactly what you are looking for, but it's best to have a backup plan.

So now you have a sketch and contract in hand from two different contractors. The contracts seem easy to understand, but do you really know the small items that are missing or that you assume to be included? You choose one, he tells you to sign the contract, give him a deposit, and the start date will be held just for you. Don't believe it, no matter how nice he seems.

Case One: Renovation

I recently did a major renovation to the upstairs of my home. The contractor seemed confident and was able to work up a drawing of just what we wanted. The price was reasonable and was based upon his labor, the actual cost of materials, plus a ten percent charge for carrying costs.

It is best to have the contractor detail the services to be performed very specifically, as well as all of the potential materials that might be needed—otherwise a vague contract means it will cost at least ten to twenty-five percent over, even if no changes were made to the original plan. Trust me, the builder will explain about all of the hidden defects during renovation that require extra service and materials, which is his way of getting more money out of you.

First of all, it is okay to sign a contract with your chosen contractor, but do not give him any money up front. Some states have something called a "waiver of liens"; check it out since it could save you a lot of aggravation. If I file the waiver before all work starts, it often makes it impossible for a subcontractor to come after me if he doesn't receive payment from the primary contractor. Remember that throughout the job, I will be giving money to the contractor, not the subcontractors, and I want to avoid being sued by a subcontractor who isn't paid by my contractor.

In this case the contractor told me I needed to give him a deposit to reserve the date. I refused. If I absolutely had to put something down, it should have been no more than $500 (so that if my contractor suddenly disappeared, all I had to lose was the $500). Many of the contracts I have been given over the years have indicated that the contractor wanted ten percent before the start of the job to purchase supplies. Well, if the contractor was that poor, maybe I was choosing the wrong person for the job!

Here is what I do to protect myself. I tell the contractor that the day he starts and puts the first materials on my property, I will gladly hand over the ten percent. (If he doesn't have some credit with a building materials supplier, then I don't want him doing my work.) In such a case, I at least have the materials equal to the dollar amount I give him just in case the contractor doesn't show the second day, which does sometimes happen. It isn't about trust—it is about protecting myself, as a consumer, against the worst-case scenarios.

My recent renovation involved redoing a bathroom. The contractor gave me his contract, showing a ten percent deposit one week before the start of the project plus three draw dates (or pay points) based upon the job itself. I said I'd give him the ten percent check at the end of the first day but he had to have most of the materials delivered to my property. He reluctantly agreed, which means I won that round.

He also required a one-third draw after the old fixtures were totally removed, another one-third when the reconstruction was half-finished (whatever that means) and the balance less $1,000 before the finish and during the final painting. Of course, a contractor could paint the bathroom long before installing the sinks, toilet, shower, etc., so what does "before the finish" really mean?

I protected myself by changing the draw schedule to

five or six throughout the duration of the job. Consumers should always do what is in their best interest. If the contractor really wants the job, he will agree to changing the pay periods. Set it up so the contractor can draw only after the work has been performed, never before. This will also help ensure a timely completion of your job. If the contractor has the money but has not completed the work, he will tend to pull his crew to another job to get paid and let me, the consumer, sit. By controlling the money distribution, I am in a better position to control the pace of the job itself. The rule of thumb is if the contractor wants his money, let him finish the next stage.

The bathroom was finally completed and I owed another $4,200 to the contractor. I've mentioned that this job was based on a labor contract plus materials with a ten percent add-on. Well, there were three major items listed for which the contractor could not account. However, I had set it up that the contractor could not collect that balance from me until he produced his actual invoices and I verified them. So what does that tell me about the contractor? He most likely bought these items at a reduced price and expected me to pay retail cost. If I had seen the true invoice, however, I would have paid no more than cost plus ten percent.

It took slightly over two years for my contractor to produce the documentation I required. From the completion of the job until that time, I retained the final payment. Once I verified the cost of the three items in question, I gladly paid the final invoice.

Case Two: Missing Materials

Many years ago, I hired a contractor to do some major landscaping due to a water problem in and around the outside of my house. I signed the contract with all of the specifications clearly described. However, before the work actually started, I knew enough to file a "waiver of liens" in my state.

As the work proceeded, the contractor kept coming to me every few days to say he needed more materials than he thought so I had to sign off on the additions. I did this knowing what was being ordered and what costs were being added.

Finally, when the project was completed, I was presented with a bill showing the specific materials list and the final balance due. Before rushing to give him a check, I asked for a few days to review everything. Then I compared the materials list with the actual items used on the job and found some major discrepancies. When I approached the contractor, he denied any wrongdoing but I refused to pay him the balance until he could verify everything.

He ended up trying to sue me for final payment. I went to court and explained to the judge (no jury) exactly what I had noticed, and that I had also found out that my contractor was simultaneously doing another job in another neighborhood using similar materials. I brought detailed pictures of the work done on my property and I also hired an independent contractor to review my contract and make an assessment of the materials used. His evaluation supported mine and he noted the materials that were missing.

Since this was in a small town, the judge actually came to my property to look for himself. His verdict? The contractor was wrong and the materials were missing. The contractor ended up not only forfeiting the balance I owed him, but was sanctioned by the court to return some money to me for other materials I had already paid for—and his contractor's license was suspended within the county.

This only goes to show how important it is to keep an eye on the work being done (or hire an independent contractor to assess it for you). Don't be intimidated by contractors. Be assertive and make sure you get exactly what you pay for.

Case Three: Walk Through

When buying a new house, just before settlement, the builder sometimes gives an opportunity to do what is called a "walk through." The purpose is to see if there is anything the builder needs to rectify after settlement. I understand that most builders take months to complete this punch-out list, especially if it is filled with items that seem unimportant. If you are knowledgeable, you can do this walk through yourself; if not, hire an expert. It is well worth it.

My first new house was purchased twenty-five years ago. As is customary, a week before settlement I was asked to do the walk through. Since I know quite a lot about building (having built a couple of structures myself), I went to this walk through armed. I took my tool belt with screwdrivers, knife blades, hammer, tape measure, etc.

Most people walk around room by room with the contractor's representative showing them such things as a scrape in the paint, something that's coming loose, chips in the plaster, and issues of a similar nature. The important things are totally missed because the average homebuyer does not know what to look for.

I used my walk through to open all sealed walls, get into crawlspaces, look under sinks for plumbing concerns, check wiring circuits, and so on. What I found was amazing! Insulation was missing in the attic, pipes exposed to the outside were not insulated and would be subject to freezing in the winter, outlets in the walls did not work, wallboards were not secure, and there were plumbing errors of major proportion. As a result, I generated seven pages of punch-out items instead of the usual half page. I knew what to look for; that is why it may be a good idea to hire a home inspector to go with you.

Many of these problems might not have been discovered for years and the builder sure wasn't going to come back to fix them! Repairs would have been at my expense. I think the builder respected what I did on the walk through because everything on my seven pages was fixed within two weeks while many of my neighbors were still calling for repairs eight months later.

This is one situation that definitely requires an aggressive and knowledgeable approach. Otherwise…buyer, beware!

Case Four: Rebuilding the Kitchen

I already mentioned having to rebuild my entire water-damaged kitchen, for which I was able to negotiate with a local kitchen rebuilder for new cabinets, floor and installation. When the work was to begin, the owner of the company showed up wanting money before anyone started. I said I'd give him the first of six draws at the end of day one on the job, when the old oven and flooring were removed.

Initially the kitchen company was to use a high-level, qualified installer but he quit, so they sent another installer who was so old and out of shape that I was afraid he was going to expire on the job. Actually, the gentleman was not going to do any of the work himself but was going to direct some laborers he must have hired that day.

After the old items were removed, I gave the owner of the kitchen company the first draw and agreed to give him the second one when all of the new cabinets were in my garage. Naturally, he made sure they were there the next day. (Those cabinets were worth more than the first two draws.)

Again, knowing something about building, I asked the installer to install all the base cabinets on one-fourth-inch plywood strips. This would raise them slightly and, after the tile floor was installed, would make it easier to slide a dishwasher in and out of its space.

Things began to go downhill from there. The base cabinets were installed directly on the floor and the overhead (or hanging) cabinets were not level. The installer insisted they were straight so I got my long level and, sure enough, I was right. I called the owner of the kitchen company and, only after I halted the work, he came over and agreed to have all of the cabinets removed and installed again properly—though this didn't happen without a fight.

After the cabinets were reinstalled correctly, the old installer decided to put the sink in himself but I stopped him after he kept having trouble. Again, I called the owner and insisted he bring in a certified plumber. You do not have to accept just anyone working on your plumbing. Most cities or counties require that a certified plumber and electrician do new installations.

The doors were installed and when it came time to

drill holes for the handles, wouldn't you know it? The installer drilled them at two different levels. I called the owner, who had to order the manufacturer to ship in two new doors. Easy enough…until the installer did the same stupid thing a second time when drilling the holes! At this point, I asked the installer to gather his tools and leave my house forever. I called the kitchen store to explain why and also took it upon myself to call the manufacturer, who was kind enough to ship two new doors (in order to have good customer relations, they didn't charge me a thing). Then I hired someone else to install the doors and drill the holes for the handles.

Next, the floor installer arrived. He came with fifteen years experience so I thought he must be good. Wrong again! When I returned home, I noticed that the angle of the tile was not in keeping with the diagonal design of the kitchen. It looked stupid. I told him to stop until I got the owner of the kitchen store, who had to admit that I was right once again and ordered the floor installer to remove the tiles, purchase new ones and do the job correctly.

It wasn't over yet. The floor was in place for all of three weeks when the tiles started to pop out. I made the usual calls. The installer stated that this was unusual so he reinstalled about ten of them. Again, this lasted about three weeks before the tiles were coming loose everywhere. Fortunately, I still had a large chunk of money withheld from the kitchen store. So this time I insisted that the entire floor be removed and another installer do the instillation. They refused so I fired them and hired my own contractor.

It turned out the original instillation was performed without a special adhesive in the cement, so it was inevitable that the floor would come loose.

This is when it really gets good…and this is how I stood up for my rights! I took the kitchen company to court for gross incompetence and the use of non-county-approved labor. Overall, the cost for me to complete the job using another contractor totaled around $4,500.

After only fifteen minutes of hearing the story, the judge found for me and ordered that I be paid the $4,500 plus all court costs. The kitchen company owner refused to pay so it was essential that I knew which remedies were available through the courts. I filed an execution of the judgment, which meant that after forty-five days without word from the kitchen store owner, I was able to file with the sheriff's office to serve the company directly and claim all of the property in the store for sale by the sheriff.

The sheriff went into the store with proper documents and started placing large red stickers, marked "Sheriff's Sale," on all the cabinets. After a call to the owner's lawyer, the sheriff received a check for my money and all court costs involved. The owner paid to stop the sheriff from tagging everything and seizing his showroom cabinets.

The moral of the story is that consumers must sometimes rely on the local courts. Ask questions and you will be amazed how helpful they can be. The court clerks walked me through every step of the process until I reached the end and received justice. Sure, it took time (eight months and two court appearances, to be exact) but the end result was more than worth it.

Chapter 10

Learning About Lemon Laws

Remember the days when either you or someone you knew complained about having an automobile that was considered a "lemon"? This still happens, of course, but most people no longer know how to fight the dealers to reach an agreeable resolution. Consumers think they have to live with the problem or get rid of the car and move on. But that isn't the answer since most states have "lemon laws"—and they do work. How do I know? Simple. I have successfully returned two vehicles.

Case One: Returning a Vehicle

The first case was a 1992 car that had its first transmission failure at only 1,200 miles, leaving me stranded inside a tunnel and holding up traffic for over two hours. At first I thought it was a fluke so after it was repaired, I went on my way thinking that everything should be all right. Over the next ten months, the transmission was rebuilt three times (so much for optimism!) and the car had brake failure, needed the shocks replaced twice and had countless other problems.

Frustrated, I thought of trading in the vehicle even though it would have meant a loss of about $5,000. That's probably what most people would have done to stop throwing good money after bad. Instead, I looked into the lemon laws, which were new at the time, and decided to find out how to apply for the return of the vehicle. After about twenty phone calls, this best-kept secret was out of the bag and I now understood how to apply. It would involve completing several papers and sending in supporting documents.

I did exactly as required and sent the originals of every document I had. (Always make copies of everything in case something is conveniently lost or put in the big circular file by accident.) It took only ninety days for them to send me the answer that I did not qualify for the return.

Now I was angry since the transmission failed again and there was only a little more than 16,000 miles on the vehicle. I started the process over and was once again turned down.

My next try was more successful because, with the help

of a dealer, I was able to show the review board the actual repair costs to the manufacturer over the time I had the vehicle. The total ranged from $4,500 - $4,700. After the ninety-day period, I received a letter telling me to pick out any new vehicle in the dealership. If the price was exactly the same as my original price, I would only have to pay a hundred dollars for the transfer of the plates.

However, what I also learned was that the manufacturer had the right to reverse the title within various states and the vehicle would be listed as having never been registered. In this way, it could be sold at an auction and some unsuspecting consumer would inherit my old car and its inherent problems. There was nothing I could do about that—but I sure did hope that the person had heard about lemon laws!

I picked another model and ended up paying an additional $550 in price difference plus the hundred, and drove away with a new vehicle. This entire process only took about fifteen months. Being assertive and staying on top of the situation allowed me to achieve the result I wanted without an attorney being involved.

And you know what they say about turning lemons into lemonade!

Case Two: Manufacturer's Defect

In the late 1990s, my son purchased his very first car with the money he earned from his own business, which he started at the age of twelve. It was his dream car—but the dream was shattered as he hit the 1,400-mile mark. The engine started to leak oil and the dealer couldn't stop the leak. It turned out that the entire block had been manufactured with a warp in it and a new engine was needed.

I already had experience in returning one car so I decided that this one also had to go. Naturally, the dealership already had its money and was not going to do anything to help, although they agreed to continue fixing the vehicle, no matter how many times it took. (The dealer would receive payment for this from the manufacturer since it was outside the realm of minor adjustments.) But who wanted a car that was always in for repairs?

A factory representative looked at the vehicle and agreed that the engine was bad. My concern was that my sixteen-year-old son could break down while driving his first-ever car and I didn't want him stranded somewhere without help (this was before the days of cell phones). The manufacturer's representative referred me to the regional office.

I called the regional office and explained the concerns I had as a father. I also mentioned that if they couldn't do something fair, this teenager would most likely never purchase another vehicle from them over his lifespan and would make sure that everyone he knew found out why.

I was directed to apply for the return of the vehicle and

completed the paperwork. This process took only thirty days and I received a letter to pick out a new car. My son decided to go with the same make and model but it had to be ordered. The regional office was able to speed up the process and the car arrived within three weeks.

I guess this sounded simple. Well, it was…until we realized that the new car came without cruise control. The manufacturer's representative said it could be retrofit and added to the vehicle by one of their aftermarket installers. The work would carry the full backing of the manufacturer. We agreed, so everyone was happy…for the time being.

About a month after the installation, my son was in school when everyone came running out to the parking lot to see a car on fire. Care to guess whose car it was? Yep, my son's. The cruise control had shorted and was too close to the fuel line so the entire vehicle burned.

We called the regional manufacturer's office and explained the details. They were stunned and sent out the field representative. The manufacturer was going to make good by allowing my son to pick out another new car but he wanted me to use my insurance to subrogate against the manufacturer and they, in turn, were going to subrogate against the installer of the cruise control. I left that mess up to everyone else involved.

Although it sounds complicated, it really wasn't for

us. My son had installed his own sunroof and spoiler so the manufacturer agreed to include these items in the newest version, and said it would take a total of about ninety-five days to drive away with it.

However, the insurance company wanted to depreciate the value of the last vehicle even though it only had around 2,200 miles on it. I'm sure they would have gotten the full value when they subrogated and would have made a nice profit on my situation. I read the insurance regulations, insisted they replace the vehicle with a like-for-like one and refused the money. I wanted the exact same car with all of the options in the same color, though I'd be willing to accept a used one with up to 6,000 miles. I told the insurance company to check all around the country and find me one. Believe it or not, most insurance policies indicate that they will either give you a check or a replacement. I wanted the replacement, which really put their feet to the fire.

After two weeks, I received a call from the company that a like vehicle couldn't be found and I would have to go the other route. I refused and told them to replace it. In the meantime, we were using a rental vehicle, which was costing the insurance company eighteen dollars a day, so I was in no hurry.

Forty-eight hours later, I received a call from the head adjuster authorizing the purchase of the new vehicle with every option and waiving the deductible. The insurance company was going to pay the full invoice with nothing out of my pocket.

Insurance companies will do anything to get you, the insured, to do exactly what is in their best interest; they are only concerned with their loss ratios. Read your policy carefully before you call so that you know exactly what you are entitled to. Being informed will make it easier to get a positive outcome, as I did, and get you back in the driver's seat.

Chapter 11

The Deal With Credit Card Disputes

C redit cards want your business so they make you attractive deals and promises up front; this all changes when you try to use those services. That's when the fine details of your one-sided contract surface.

Disputing a charge on your credit card seems simple enough but it is not so. Remember, the credit card company makes most of its money from other companies that are merchants. A perfect example is an airline that pays the credit card company millions of dollars a year in business; it may seem like the credit card company is trying to help the consumer's cause, but it really sides with the airline when there is a dispute.

Case One: Dispute Resolution Team

Recently, I had to dispute a charge on one of my credit cards and the dispute resolution department was very courteous and helpful. They took the information in detail and were very sympathetic to my plight. The conversation ended with a temporary credit while the situation was turned over to their internal investigation team. I really felt good about their attitude and figured I knew I was in the right and that my card company was there for me. How wrong I was!

Two weeks passed and I received a letter asking me to send the details of the dispute within ten days or the case would be dropped. This was the first hint that the credit card company was looking for a way to make this go away. I stared at the letter wondering why I had spent thirty minutes on the phone giving details to the dispute resolution department if the team now had no idea what the dispute was about.

The next step was to put everything about the dispute in writing and include any supporting documentation that might have been helpful. Doing my due diligence, I put together my letter and sent the packet explaining everything I could in accurate and precise detail.

Another ten days went by and I received another letter indicating that the inquiry had been sent to the merchant. It also asked if, in the meantime, I had tried to contact the merchant to see if I could get some resolution. I responded that I did try and it is for this reason that I was now asking for dispute resolution from the credit card company since the merchant refused to negotiate. Thinking I would receive a favorable decision from the dispute team was definitely a wrong assumption. Another two or three weeks went by and I got another form letter from them stating that the merchant sent some enclosed documentation and all of the copies were included with the letter to me. The dispute resolution team never reviewed the documents; the papers sent by the merchant were accepted on blind faith and there really wasn't any dispute resolution at all. The final sentence of the letter stated that my card was going to be charged for the product or service that I disputed.

Note that at no time did anyone in the dispute department indicate that they read my information and reviewed the merchant's information in an effort to arbitrate a decision. All they did was collect documents from me and the merchant, then immediately take the merchant's side because they sent in some paperwork. All they really looked at was the bottom line: the merchant's business with them may have meant thousands or millions in revenue, whereas I, the card holder, amounted to peanuts.

So what could I do other than take it on the chin and give up? Fight the system that just walked all over me!

My next action was to send a lengthy letter to the card dispute team restating my original case and flatly accusing them of not really having reviewed the merits of the situation but simply taking the side of the merchant. This letter got the attention of the person I had been working with and was sent on to a higher level (which is what I wanted to happen). While waiting for a response, I also called to start the dispute all over again.

After ten days, I received a letter from a different person inside the dispute department indicating that they would look further into the problem and request a response from the merchant. Now, I was getting somewhere. It was the first time the card company was actually making an effort to look at the story from both sides.

What had just happened here was that my dispute had been elevated to the next level. In some cases, the merchant will simply agree to issue a permanent credit because it is too time-consuming to keep writing back and forth. Other times, the merchant offers a compromise that can be agreeable to both parties, such as a new product or a reduction in cost. Still other times, the merchant will stand fast.

When the merchant stands fast, you must do the same and keep the ball rolling. Don't let the merchant or the credit card company off the hook until something gives. This will often get the merchant to call you directly to find some middle ground since the chargeback has taken money from their system, leaving an open account receivable. I have worked at these problems for up to eight months after starting the process. Larger companies or merchants do not like having aging accounts since the value of the dollar is decreasing. They will often settle for a lesser percentage just to make you go away and close the books.

I stressed the fact that I was willing to go to court to ask a judge to make the decision, and that it would cost them more time and money to answer my complaint that way.

Case Two: Disputing an Airline Charge

Think I can't win against the airlines and their no-refund or exchange policies? Think again. Yes, airlines are insulated against chargebacks because credit card companies are afraid of losing the millions in revenue they make from those airlines. But it is not impossible to win a dispute.

Some time ago, I scheduled travel with a large airline carrier for a specific date and time. If I made any changes to my reservation, I stood the possibility of forfeiting the entire fare or, if allowable, I could change the ticket within a year but with $100 in penalties. So why wouldn't it work the other way around? Well, in a sense it would, but I had to stand fast and be willing to fight back.

I booked those tickets to get to a noon meeting in

another city. My two-hour flight was scheduled to leave at 8 a.m., but seventy-two hours before the flight, the airline changed the departure to 11 a.m. I had to cancel my plans, but the airline didn't want to refund my money.

Fortunately, I was able to cancel the meeting and my hotel arrangements without any penalty. I guess the airlines alone feel that they have us where they want us— and what are we going to do about it?

I will let you in on my secret of how to handle this situation. First, I filed a dispute with my credit card company, even though they did not want to get involved. The credit card company told me that the airlines have rules that must be honored from the onset. But I didn't take no for an answer. I let them know that I had rights under consumer protection laws and would expect them to hold charges until the matter was settled in court. I forced them by a treat of suit to help in the resolution process. I wasn't afraid of them.

Next, I wrote a letter to the airline outlining the particulars and made it clear that if they did not give me the credit, I would ask the F.A.A. to get involved and, out of principle, would take this to court. The airlines didn't care what I intended to do until it actually happened. Therefore, I "cc"ed the letter to the F.A.A. and included a letter that was written directly to the F.A.A. with the airline's first notice. In such cases, sometimes it will work and there will be a response indicating that the credit has been issued; other times the airline will stand its ground, assuming the consumer will not be going to do anything to take it a step further.

If they don't resolve the issue then you must proceed. Go to the airline's website and get the name of the CEO; you can also often find the state of incorporation. Many airlines, like most large corporations, use Delaware when creating their corporate structures. Call the state of incorporation and they will help with the name and address of the resident agent. When all of this is in place, you often have the right to create the suit in small claims court within your state, but not always. Calling the local court will often help. Large corporations doing business in your state often register as a "foreign corporation."

In my case, I filed the claim and wrote a short paragraph about the suit and the amount requested. When I filed the claim, the court asked if I wanted the service to be by certified mail or by a sheriff. In this case, I had service sent to two locations: the resident agent and the CEO of the company.

Ninety-nine percent of the time, this action will get a call from someone at the airline indicating that a credit will be issued. Answering the suit would cost the airline too much time and money, and doing what I did told them that I meant business. Most people would be happy to simply accept the credit, but not me. I asked the airline to pay my fifteen or thirty dollars in court costs also (they usually will because they cannot believe anyone would have the gumption to take this type of action).

Finally, there is a rule that if the airline changes your reservation by a couple of hours, they are obligated to give you a refund (though they will never tell you this when the schedule is changed). Once the airline gives you a refund, you can notify the credit card dispute division that they are off the hook—but that you should have received the credit you deserved in the first place.

Watch your card company carefully. In tough situations, some will open a dispute up to six months after the item was originally charged to your account. On the other hand, many will only open a dispute within sixty days of the initial charge (supporting my theory that these companies aren't interested in the consumer, only in the merchant). It may be in your best interest to dump credit cards that have such limitations and look for ones that are more forgiving. They are definitely out there, so choose to do business with them—that is the power we have as consumers.

Chapter 12

Keep Your Cool or Get Hot Under the Collar— Problems With Heating and Air Conditioning

Think things can't get worse than dealing with general contractors? Try hassling with the heating and air conditioning industry.

For the most part, these service companies are fairly honest but as in any industry, there are those who will take advantage of the public simply because they think they can. It is hard to prove any wrongdoing, and one of the biggest culprits is the manufacturer who refuses to talk to the consumer about their units. They tend to defer any concerns or warranty problems back to an authorized dealer. So all you can do is jump from the frying pan into the fire without ever getting a straight answer.

Case One: Unit Repairs

I purchased a house on the resale market that was only two years old and had a dual zone system, one for each floor. Within the first three months, the heat pump unit broke down. Not knowing who to call, I located one of the largest service companies in my area; however, the first thing I realized about the industry was that since I didn't have a "service contract," I would be treated like a second-class citizen and placed on the bottom of the list for a service call. It didn't matter that I was a new customer and this company may have wanted to win my business. I was still considered a low-life bottom-dweller and would be treated as such.

Two days went by and someone finally showed up—unannounced. I guess they expected me to take off from work and sit home to be present if and when they decided to drop by and fix my unit. No one was home when they came so they left, called me and scheduled an appointment for two days later. (It was almost like dealing with an airline's customer service department, where customers don't really count.) This country has no idea what the true meaning of service is. We, the people, are necessary for the survival of many companies, but only if we do it their way.

The glorious day arrived and the service technician showed up only thirty minutes late. Not too bad, I guess, considering. He checked the unit and came downstairs to tell me that my condensing coil was rusty and leaking—on a two-and-a-half-year-old unit! It could be covered under warranty, he suggested, but the circuit board was also bad. This board cost $400 and was not covered by the warranty. Did I know if the board was really gone? Of course not, but I was relying on the technician to be honest. Little did I know that the industry prided itself on cheating people to make a living.

Having an infant at home and being in the midst of the hot summer season, I had no choice but to allow him to proceed. What could I do—get another opinion? Then he told me that none of the parts were in stock so it wouldn't be fixed for another two days. I have never figured out if that was really true or if he figured that time is money and moved on to another job for the day.

Two days later, the technician showed up, replaced the condensing coil and the circuit board and charged the unit with new refrigerant. This sounded above-board enough…until I got the bill and found an extra service charge. Since the temperature on the day that the technician finally decided to do the repair was over 110 degrees in the attic, I had an extra charge for him having to work in the heat. Could he have come in the evening when it was cooler? Sure, but why would he want to do that? At that point, I had lost enough time from work so I simply paid the bill and went back to my job.

About four months later, the heat pump failed again so I called the same company, thinking they must have done something wrong and that the work was covered by their own warranty. Not surprisingly, however, it turned out that the problem was caused by something different. It seems that when they gassed the unit on the last visit, the technician left the cap off the inlet valve and the unit had to be re-gassed. I was presented with another bill, so I paid it. But, later, I called customer service and a representative explained that since the unit was serviced by them four months ago and the gas didn't leak during the first ninety days, it was no longer their problem, even if their worker did leave the cap off. Again, my time was too important to worry about it at that point.

Well, what do you know? Two months went by and the unit broke down again. This time the technician couldn't figure out what was wrong; he knew that the problem was somewhere in the low voltage system, so he ordered one part after another until he hit upon, by sheer dumb luck, the correct part to replace. This process took eleven days until the unit was repaired and working again. My bill reflected all the time that he spent at my house and all the parts that were ordered, even those that didn't need to be replaced and were. What is wrong with this picture? He was supposed to be the expert and I ended up paying for his mistakes. Remember, this was the largest company in the area.

Another month went by and again there was another breakdown. Since it was fall and I now had a service contract for $369 in place for the unit (I am not sure what that meant since I ended up paying every time they came to my house anyway), I called my contracted company. This time the knowledgeable technician told me that this three-and-a-half-year-old unit was shot and should be replaced. By then, I had put close to $2,000 of my money into heating and air conditioning.

I decided it was smarter to change everything for a new type of unit and receive a full labor and service warranty for ten years. In the long run, it was cheaper doing it that way.

With the help of a friend, I used another contractor, who was very straightforward and told me he could potentially fix the unit but suggested replacing everything, including the duct work. I agreed. After all, how many times could I go to the same company that fixed the unit until it broke again? Maybe the unit was a lemon, but trying to call the manufacturer about their warranty got me no place. They simply turned the issue back to the repair company.

All was well until the next fall, when the original repair company, which still had my lower heating system under extended warranty, returned to do a check-up. It had been working perfectly and producing heat without any problem. Still, the technician went into my basement and, after tinkering around, came up and told my wife that the filter in the one-year-old humidifier needed to be replaced. She authorized that service, figuring it was no problem. Well, she spoke too soon. After another twenty minutes, he came up from the basement and informed her that the lower heating unit was not working due to a cracked circuit board. She called me at work and I authorized the repair, but I couldn't believe that all of these problems were starting over again with the second system.

Something seemed to be amiss since the problems always occurred when this company came into my house to either repair or check my unit. Fortunately, they had nothing to do with the one upstairs any longer.

Three days went by before the board was available for installation. This time, the service technician showed up along with a chief technician, who had been with the company for twenty-five years. Either the service technician was too new or didn't know what he was doing so he needed to have another technician present. Interestingly, he had taken my old board out of the house while waiting for the new one to arrive, and I had suspected foul play. I called and told him to bring back my board, so maybe that was the reason the head technician came with him.

Sure enough, the new board was installed and the unit didn't work. It turned out that it was nothing more than a bad thermostat to begin with. I requested that they put the old board back and take the new one with them. The chief technician explained that the old board was broken, showing me a crack in the plastic. I paid my bill and after they left, decided to go a step further. I was suspicious that they were simply changing parts and probably getting a percentage bonus for every one they sold since labor was covered under my yearly maintenance program.

I used to build radio equipment and work with electronics so I ran some tests on the old board myself. The crack they had shown me was in a plastic retainer that had nothing to do with the function of the board itself (the plastic shelf simply retained a "common" [ground] screw from shorting anything else on the board). The average layperson believes technicians; we expect these service people to be honest and fair. What consumers do not bargain for is the dishonest company that teaches its employees to break things in order to make bonus money on parts.

It appeared that a small section of plastic had been broken by a screwdriver that was too large for the opening when the thermostat wires were removed the first time. The technician put too much pressure on the plastic, so it had to fracture.

I did one more step to verify what I suspected. I removed the new circuit board and re-installed the old one. It worked perfectly. This confirmed that I was being taken advantage of by the company. I decided to strike back. But how?

First, I called the county office that handles contractors' licensing and obtained a complaint form to file, asking for the county to do an investigation. This was not enough so I planned my next attack. I decided to raise a dispute on my credit card, which would get them involved. Even that wasn't enough. I also planned to bring action in court, which only cost fifteen dollars to file the case.

My decision to let a court hear the case was one of the most effective things I could do. I was undertaking this without an attorney but decided I would subpoena the CEO of the company, the service manager, the head technician and the technician who arrived in the first place. If necessary, I was willing to hire an expert on my side, but decided I really didn't need one. Win or lose, I would cost the company a lot of money by subpoenaing all four employees into court and most likely causing the CEO to hire an attorney for thousands of dollars.

Next, I wrote a lengthy letter to the CEO explaining much of what had happened and sent it by certified mail to make sure it was received. I told him that my attorney recommended I contact him about this situation before I took further action, even though I never consulted with my attorney.

Four days went by and I got a call from the company's

division service manager. I purposely waited one day before returning the call then briefly went over a few of my points about the company's service during the past year and a half. I reviewed the things that happened with my upstairs unit, the $2,000 I had spent on their company before replacing the entire system and, finally, how this perfectly good, working lower unit stopped working after their technician was at my house for only one hour.

I strongly recommend that you be prepared to let someone know exactly what you want before you discuss it with them. I told the service manager I wanted a full credit for the circuit board and he tried to excuse it away. I then informed him that the old circuit board had been checked and appeared to be functioning perfectly. At first he tried to get me to pay half the cost of the new board, but I refused.

He agreed to the credit, but wanted to send over a technician to take back the newer board. I said I would never allow them to come back into my house since every time his people touched any of my heating and air conditioning units, something seemed to break. He wasn't very happy to hear that and reiterated that he wanted his board back. I told him I would agree to give him the old board instead, but that no one would touch my unit again unless it broke. They had done enough damage and this was the price they should pay for bad business and dishonesty.

We were at a standoff, so this is where I had to become more assertive. I stressed that if he didn't give me the credit without my returning the board, I was prepared to file in court and would subpoena him, the owner and both technicians, costing them hundreds of dollars to fight this claim even if I didn't prevail. He said he'd get back to me in twenty-four hours.

Sure enough, he called the next day and, I guess after talking with the CEO, agreed to give me the full credit, and the balance of my two-month service contract was cancelled.

What I can tell you is not to be afraid to back a large company into a corner if you feel you were truly wronged. The large companies, whoever they are, feel they can push people around because of their size and finances. However, the system was designed for *your* protection. Yet it is so cumbersome that most consumers just walk away and allow companies to keep stepping all over them—and that really gets me heated!

Chapter 13

The Truth About Shipping Insurance and Rebates

All of us ship packages from time to time and expect the item we ship to be protected by the insurance we purchase. It doesn't matter if it's with the United Postal Service, UPS, Fed Ex, etc. After the item is weighed, we are usually asked its value and if we want to purchase extra insurance in hopes that if the item is lost or damaged, we will be paid to replace it.

Case One:

A number of years ago I shipped a very expensive item with one of those companies and totally insured its full value. I left the facility feeling confident that my item was covered. Little did I know that my confidence would soon be shattered.

A few days later I received a call from the store where the item was being sent indicating that my package hadn't yet been received. I went back to the point of shipment and requested the item be tracked and located. They told me not to worry; it should be there within a few more days. After five more days, it still hadn't arrived.

I returned again to request a form for a lost item and they said they'd first do an internal trace to see what happened to it. Two weeks went by and back to the facility I went. After a couple of internal phone calls and another thirty minutes of my time, I was told to fill out a lost item form for processing. The problem was that I had a lot of money sitting on my credit card and had to pay the bill while the shipper was fooling around, trying to find my item.

Weeks went by and they were still investigating. I got another call ten days later that they located the item in the city where it was being shipped. I asked to see who signed for the package every point of the way and was denied that information. It was now nearing almost two months since I shipped the item in the first place.

I threatened legal action since the shipping company was playing with me. Two more weeks had passed and they still produced nothing. If they had located the item a few weeks earlier, as they had stated, then why hadn't it been delivered? I filed in small claims court against this major company after I found out who was its resident agent. The suit was about not receiving the value of my item according to my insurance coverage, but the company was denying that the item was lost so they were refusing to make payment.

Once the company received the service notification of my action, I received a call from the corporate office asking me to verify my item with a receipt. I had the store send me a current receipt and submitted it in a letter, also making it clear that I would not stop the legal action until I received a check for the full value of the item lost, the interest I lost on my money since I had to pay for the item on my credit card, and the fifteen dollars it cost me to file the claim in court.

About ten days later I received a letter and a check for the full amount of the item. This entire process took a little over three months. By the way, I did not receive my interest or the fifteen dollars for court costs, so I sent back a letter letting them know that I still intended to continue the court proceedings, knowing it would cost them much more than the roughly thirty-two dollars I was seeking. Five days later, I received a check for thirty-two dollars.

The lesson is that even though you think you are protected by insurance, these companies will do everything possible not to pay the claim. Stay on them and get everything you are entitled to. If the company can't be fair and reasonable, then neither should you be.

As a side note, having lost something insured with the U.S. Postal Service, I found them to be twice as difficult to receive a fair and timely payment from.

Case Two: Rebates

Remember a time when an item on sale really meant that it was on sale? You went to the store, purchased that item and walked out with a receipt in hand showing the discount.

Today, a sale often means a mail-in rebate, which means eight to ten weeks to get your money, if it ever comes. I go to a store, buy an item and receive an extra register receipt and rebate slip. Sounds easy enough, but is it? I have dealt with many rebates over the years that have never come. What could I do about it? Read on.

I filled out the form exactly as requested. I never sent the material to the rebate center until I made a copy of everything being sent, even the UPC from the package. This duplication was my only form of record.

With most rebates, for some reason it takes between six to ten weeks for them to pay. Most are honest deals and the rebates do show up, but there are some disreputable rebate companies. These people play games like sending back original material six weeks later with the UPC label missing, stating that they never received it. It is for this reason I put three staples into everything when I send it. Making a copy of everything I originally send gives me proof to send back to the rebate company.

In one instance, the rebate company refused to accept the copy since the original was required. This was just an excuse not to pay. Many consumers will accept this loss and simply move on, but not me. I went back to the store of purchase, got the manager and let him know the problem with the rebate company (which often has nothing to do with the store where you bought it). In some cases the managers themselves will call the company and try to get them to issue the rebate. If that doesn't work, I find that rather than have to receive the item back as a return, the store manager will usually give me a refunded discount equal to the rebate. Either way, I get what I wanted and expected in the first place.

Don't be afraid to threaten to return an item; often, the manager will make the adjustment. However, some managers are stupid and do nothing so I return the item and purchase it elsewhere, even if I can no longer get a rebate. If it involves electronics, the store will discount it and put it on a shelf or table the next day. I can go back and repurchase the same item for a lot less than the rebate was worth.

Make a statement to these stores! The more consumers do that, the more the store will become responsive to its customers.

Chapter 14

Challenging Comprehensive Coverage

Almost all of us carry comprehensive insurance with different levels of deductibles. In all the years I have been a driver, I have always had a fifty-dollar deductible, but for the past twenty years I changed to $100 per incident. This was workable for me and my family.

Case One: Changing Coverage

When my son was in high school, he made enough money on his own to purchase a new vehicle at the age of sixteen. Naturally, I agreed to carry the insurance.

During the first year that he owned the car, he was concerned about keeping it as new and pristine as the day it left the showroom. Every time someone opened a door and put a dent in his side or a stone cracked his front windshield, he would call the insurance company, pay the $100 himself and get the problem repaired.

When my policy came due, the insurance company sent a letter to me as the policy holder. It stated that they decided to change my deductible to $500 instead of the $100 I had been carrying for years since there had been three incidents in a one-year span. A lot of people who received this letter would be intimidated by the enormity of the insurance company and simply agree to the change. I did not. I took action.

I immediately called my state insurance commission to register my complaint and the person who took the report opened an investigation. For the next six weeks, I heard nothing. Finally I received a letter from the commission informing me that under the state law, the insurance company did not have the right to change the deductible on my comprehensive unless I requested it.

A copy of the determination was sent to my company and I received a letter from them correcting the problem retroactive to the policy's anniversary date. The point is not to accept what the company states as fact and to never be afraid to question their motives.

Chapter 15

Protect Yourself Against Noise Pollution

What I am about to describe has been a running battle for almost twelve years, when I first moved into a lovely area miles from any large or local airports. There was a time when I used to fly my own airplane but have not done so for twenty-five years. Fortunately for me, that experience in flying helped; however, most people would be at a total loss in the same situation, so let me show you what to do.

Case One: Dealing with the F.A.A.

It all happened when my quiet little neighborhood became part of a flight path for traffic reporters. Three local news stations decided to put small planes in the air each morning to report the traffic. The problem was that each of these aircraft followed the same flight path and flew extremely low over my house as early as 5:30 a.m. It sounded like someone was landing a plane in my backyard.

I tried calling the different news stations to explain my problem to the program directors and even sent them letters so it would be in writing. Two of the directors never acknowledged my concerns and the third indicated that there was nothing he could do. I guess it didn't matter since it wasn't happening over *their* houses. The one who bothered answering explained that it was necessary to report the morning and evening traffic from the air and flying directly over the highway itself did not give a clear view of what was happening below. Therefore, the pilots were instructed to fly at a path beside the highway so the reporters could see better.

This was totally unacceptable. When I bought my house a few years earlier, there were no little planes flying overhead. Our city has noise restrictions and I had to find a way to get them enforced. In some cases, these planes were flying so close to my house that I could actually see the pilot inside.

Sure, one solution would be to ignore the noise and keep my windows shut all the time, even in the spring or fall when the weather was mild. I did have another choice, though. I decided to review the flight regulations and see if I could find some form of violation.

I ordered flight maps for my area so I could figure out what was considered regulated air space and what was not (this was pre-9/11, so many of the rules in place today did not apply then). I went online and researched the FARs (the federal aviation regulations) by the Federal Aviation Administration, by which all pilots must comply.

Almost six months after I started the process, bingo! I found a couple of regulations that I thought the pilots were violating. With my flight maps in front of me and looking at the airspace around my location, I realized that these pilots had to fly low over my house in order to stay under the 1,000-foot level of the radar in the next three-quarters of a mile. In this way, they could utilize visual flight rules and not have to participate in the airport radar system in the immediate area.

In order to go from 1,500 to 1,000 feet in such a short distance, the pilots had to drop altitude quickly just before reaching my house so that there would not be any error causing them to fly into controlled air space. However, one of the federal aviation regulations required the pilots to maintain no less than a 1,000-foot elevation over the highest point above the roof of my house, which was not being done. I proved it by getting a set of binoculars that registered distances and was able to verify the height of the planes.

The next thing I found was a law requiring the pilots to stay a certain distance away from all radio towers. Behind my house is a state police barracks and the radio tower shoots straight up in the air. It seemed that, according to my calculations, they were all flying much too close to the radio tower.

What should I do with this information? Easy—contact the F.A.A. This large government bureaucracy is in place to protect the public but with such a complicated system, it becomes almost impossible to access. My first phone call did get a response, however, and I received a very complicated complaint form along with a booklet on how and why to file.

I waded through the minutiae and filled in the form in detail. There was only one problem with the form: Near the end, it required me to list the make and model of the aircraft along with the identification numbers painted on the plane. If I had never piloted an airplane, how was I supposed to know the make and model off the top of my head? It appeared the F.A.A. was making it impossible for the average citizen to file a complaint right from the onset.

In a few cases, the numbers of the planes are painted on the underside of the wings, but in many cases, such as mine, they are quite small and are on the tail section of a plane cruising at 120 - 140 miles per hour.

Luckily, I was able to get the make and model of the

aircraft because of my flying experience. But I soon came to the next hurdle, which was the ID numbers. Sometime over the years, the F.A.A. had allowed manufacturers to paint the numbers on the tail, which meant the only way to read them would be by standing next to the plane when it was on the ground. In the case of all three aircraft, the numbers were not visible to the naked eye.

I completed the form and sent it to the F.A.A., explaining about not being able to see the numbers. They sent me a letter stating that without that information, they could do nothing (even though I told them which TV and radio stations were using the planes and the locations where the planes were parked). They could have made a couple of phone calls and gotten the information, but they refused.

It was now almost eleven months since the problem had started. I figured those F.A.A. inspectors had only one job, which was to report to work every day, receive their paychecks and run as much interference as they could with resident complaints. Doing that is what they considered doing their job. But things only got worse from there.

I went to the regional airport and waited for each of the small aircraft to land after its morning run. When they parked in their respective areas, I went to have a polite conversation with the pilots, being the old pilot that I was. This gave me an opportunity to get the exact make and model of each aircraft, the names of the pilots and the ID numbers off each plane. I thought it was quite clever.

So the very next day, I took the copies of my original three complaint forms, filled in the identification numbers and filed them with the F.A.A. again. I waited another six weeks and nothing happened, so I called and was told that they had just received the complaint and it would take another six weeks for a response. To this day, I have not figured out where my letters were hidden for the first six weeks, since I had a postal receipt showing that they were actually received three days after I sent them. Who knows? Maybe they first had to send them to the South Pole in order to get them into the hands of an inspector. In any case, I was afraid of dying from old age before the F.A.A. got around to doing its job.

Weeks went by and I finally received one of those form letters telling me that my claim had been assigned to the F.A.A. regional office in my area. I was given a number and name of whom to contact, and it seemed that my regional office was in Boston, a few hundred miles away. Still, I called and the person assigned told me that there was a mistake: I was to contact the F.A.A. regional office at Kennedy Airport in New York.

It was now almost a year and three months since the low-flying aircraft invaded my space. But onward to the New York office I went. I contacted the investigator there and explained the situation to him. He said he'd get back to me—my mistake was not asking him in which year he would return my call! After waiting a week, I called him again, and he said I needed to refresh his memory. It was then when I understood that the F.A.A. must hire investigators who spend the day standing at the water cooler. I would have thought that he made some notes when I spoke with him a week earlier, but I guess that wasn't part of his job description.

After I went through the entire situation again, he informed me that the issue belonged in the Baltimore F.A.A. region. So I asked why he couldn't have simply told me that last week and saved me some time. He had no answer.

Okay, now I finally felt as if I were getting someplace so I contacted the Baltimore office and went through the entire story one more time—only to have the investigator on the other end of the phone inform me that I had to go through the New York office at Kennedy Airport.

I guess if everyone could spin this problem fast enough and keep putting me off, they thought I might eventually give up and go away, but that is not my nature. I was angry with the entire system and how our government agency handled this situation, even though the F.A.A. is supposed to have a department to deal with such complaints.

Instead of throwing my hands up in the air in surrender,

I had to use some ingenuity. It was now almost one year and five months that the planes had been buzzing my house, so I sat down and wrote a very lengthy letter to the director of the F.A.A. and sent it certified mail with a signed receipt back to me.

It worked! About two weeks later, I received a personal call from the second in command of the F.A.A. himself. I guess they figured that if someone had the chutzpah to write to the director, then their office would answer me directly. We, as citizens, must make these people accountable for their jobs. In a sense, they are working for us.

The second in command told me that he had personally assigned my complaint to one of his lead investigators in the Baltimore region who would send me a follow-up letter with his name and direct number. The investigator would receive a copy of my letter to the director as well.

I called the investigator assigned to me and felt assured that he understood my problem, since he was also an active pilot. We made some shop talk for a while and then he said that he wanted to come to my area early one morning to verify the situation. We arranged to meet in the parking lot of a shopping center across from my house.

At the last minute, it turned out that I could not meet him, but he went to the arranged spot himself and called me the next day to say that I was absolutely correct and the pilots were way too close to my house and the police radio tower. Finally, confirmation—a year and a half from when the problem first started.

The end result was that the investigator met with twelve pilots and the directors of the radio stations involved to explain the violations. He made it clear that they had to take action immediately or there would be sanctions on their pilot licenses. (And, yes, they admitted that the excessive noise and lower altitudes were necessary to dive under the radar, as I had suspected.)

The pilots complied for quite some time but after about fourteen months, one plane started doing the same thing again. I contacted my newfound friend at the F.A.A. in Baltimore and he immediately called the company that owned the plane. It turned out that there was a new pilot who didn't know about the situation or the rules that were in place.

It is now about six years later and some of the problems have started to surface again. I am not sure if my friend has retired from the F.A.A., but I have not yet received a response as of writing this chapter. If I cannot get some answers soon, I will once again contact the director's office, which should get their attention.

Isn't it a shame that there are steps in place for a citizen to file a complaint but the system is designed to spin everything in a complete circle and to never take any action? Remember that as a citizen I am entitled to service from the government agencies so I wasn't afraid to push forward until I got some answers. I made the system work for me, the way it was intended to.

Chapter 16

Problems With Professional Services

Case One: Calling a Plumber

In everyone's life, there comes a day when you have to call a plumber. I've learned that this is a day to be dreaded. We all rely on the fact that these workers are held to certain county licensure regulations, which ensure expertise and competence—or at least that's what we hope.

During a business trip, I got a call from my wife telling me that the kitchen sink wouldn't drain and she tried everything she could think of. So I gave her the name of a plumber who had worked in our area for over thirty years and she got him to come over almost immediately.

The expert plumber looked at the sink and tried a

plunger, without any success. My wife already did that. He then proceeded to open the drain under the sink and check for a clog. Not finding any, he used a snake to see if he could open the clog further down the pipe. Nothing seemed to be working so he told my wife that he needed to send someone with a camera on the end of the snake to see if they could find the clog. He further explained that if that wasn't successful, the line in the street would have to be opened and that could get very expensive. He left and charged her for a service call anyway.

When I flew home, I asked my wife to explain exactly what she saw the plumber do. She told me, worried that the snake with the camera would cost around $500 and opening the street line would be another $3,500.

Fortunately, I consider myself smarter than the plumber and have some mechanical ability. It seemed to me that to check a stopped drain, one should start at the opening in the sink and work your way forward, not in the middle as he did. (If the clog were further in the pipe or at street level, my basement plumbing would have been blocked, which it wasn't.) I got my tools and went under the sink, completely removing the garbage disposal. This took a whole five minutes. When I looked at the side drain pipe of the disposal, I found a small piece of plastic wrapper from a fruit bag blocking the drain. I put everything back together and it has worked perfectly ever since.

I called for a professional and got someone whose error could have cost me up to $4,000 without having ever found the problem. Fortunately, that didn't happen, but I still wasn't satisfied with the service. I called the owner of the plumbing company and asked for a refund. I told him I had used his company because I thought he had professionals working for him but, in this case, the plumber didn't know his trade and should not have been left alone to do a job. He agreed, gave me the refund and indicated that he would put that plumber back in an apprentice position for a while.

I really don't know if the owner did what he said, but had I not called, he never would have known there was a problem with the service and I would not have gotten my money returned. Don't be afraid to let the owners of a company know that their workers did an unsatisfactory job. Many times all the owner sees is revenue and has no idea if the work is being done properly. My action not only got me a refund, it will help other customers in the future.

Case Two: Cable TV

Remember the service you used to get when those cable TV companies were starting and wanted your business? Like all growing companies, all they could offer at the beginning was great service. Then they grow and grow and become so successful that their service goes by the wayside. You wind up having to jump through hoops for their service rather than the company doing everything it can for its customers. The customer service department becomes arrogant and nasty because they have so many customers that there is no longer a need to be nice and courteous. They have become all-powerful and now you need them more than they need you.

Our family decided to order high definition with a recording box. All I had to do was call and place the order. I thought this first step would be easy but somehow it took the customer service department almost thirty minutes just to take the order and log the promotional offer I received in the mail. It seems the person couldn't find the offer in the system, yet I was holding the letter in my hand. My solution was to fax it over for their review, but they couldn't receive any faxes, or so I was told. I was then asked to take time off from work to bring it into the office. Would you believe that to place my order with them, they actually had the gumption to ask me to come into their office and show them the promotion, like I was supposed to be at their beck and call and have nothing better to do with my time? I refused and asked for a supervisor (whom I often refer to as a "stupidvisor" since these people are elevated to their highest level of incompetency).

The supervisor finally got involved and after five more

minutes, found the offer in the system and was now able to complete the transaction. The next step was to schedule the time for the technician to come and install the box. It makes me sick how these companies expect us, the consumer, to sit around and wait for someone to show up within a four-hour window of opportunity. Oh, well, I had to comply with their system—after all, I am only the customer who is paying the bill.

The scheduled day arrived and I waited for the technician to come between 8 a.m. and noon. Finally, at ten minutes to twelve, I received a call from the technician letting me know that he was going to be an hour and a half late and expecting me to sit around and be there at his convenience. Only the technician works for a living; everyone else just sits home all day doing nothing.

I asked the technician if he got paid for these installations. "Of course," he replied. I then asked if he thought my time wasn't worth anything. As he stumbled for words, I agreed to wait but asked him what the company was going to reimburse me. Now he was in a bind and didn't know how to answer, so I cancelled the scheduled call, indicating that I had my own life and things to do.

Then I called the cable office to reschedule, which meant that it would be another ten days. Since I am not a television nut, I thought that was acceptable, but I still wanted to know what the company was going to do for me after making me sit around for four hours for nothing. The customer service person offered me a twenty-dollar credit, which is like receiving fifteen dollars a day as a juror.

Ten days went by and again I waited for my window of opportunity. Can you guess what happened? The technician never showed then finally called at 8 p.m. to explain that his car had broken down. I said I understood and asked if he could come to my house at 8 a.m. the next morning. Do you know what he had the nerve to say? He could not do that since it was up to the scheduling department. I asked if he was nuts! Obviously, his broken down car was just an excuse because if he were half-interested in his job, he would call the scheduling department himself and go out of his way to make it happen.

The next morning, I called customer service again and all I got was, "I'm sorry but we can't send anyone out for another eight days." I asked about the idea of customer service and told the supervisor that I had to work like she did to pay for this cable, feed my family, etc. Did she really expect me to sit around again and wait for a third time? I asked why she couldn't accommodate me since it was their error twice before. She adamantly said that it wasn't company policy and there was nothing she could do.

I did want the high-def installed but since I was not in a hurry, let me show you what I did in response to their indifference. I scheduled another appointment for eight days later, and the next day, I scheduled an appointment for nine days later, then I scheduled a third one for ten days later. Since they had everything in the computer and I know that only installers do installation, I scheduled each appointment for a different reason.

The eighth day arrived, the date of installation for my new cable box. When the technician called to say he was on his way, I left the house so I wouldn't be there when he came. I did this the next day and the day after that.

Each day I missed the appointment, I called customer service to reschedule. I did this same procedure three more times so I could irritate them and cost them money by sending technicians to my home.

When I called for the fourth time, they said that each time the technician showed up, I didn't answer the door. I explained that I couldn't move quickly, which wasn't true, so by the time I got to the door the technician was gone. The customer service person understood and scheduled me for another appointment at 8 a.m., asking me to please be near the front door so I wouldn't miss the appointment again. Sometimes you have to fight fire with fire and play the game the way the company plays it—but be creative! Ultimately, I got what I wanted, which was an appointment on my time schedule.

So you think they would want to get it right, but think again. The technician hooked up the box but forgot the cables necessary for the operation. Since these technicians are paid by the job, he told me that if *I* went over to the cable office, customer service would give the audio and visual cables to me. He was willing to show me where to plug them in and said that it was really easy. This technician was really cute, expecting me to go to the cable office, stand on line for the usual thirty to forty-five minutes and do *his* job while he was getting paid and I'd be missing another two hours of work. I asked him if he was joking and insisted he unhook the equipment and get it out of my house. I told him to return when he had everything and was ready to do his job fully. He was angry, but that wasn't my problem.

I called his supervisor, who sent someone else back later in the day with everything and who managed to hook the unit up correctly this time. The rule of thumb is not to accept mediocrity and say thank you. If I stood my ground and made these service people accountable for their actions, I would get the service I was entitled to despite their attempts to do the job poorly.

Case Three: Equipment Delivery

Have you ever felt that you were being held captive by delivery people? I do every time I order something large to be delivered to my house. This could involve anything from a mattress, washer and dryer or refrigerator to a piece of exercise equipment. It seems no matter what it is and how much you are required to pay for that delivery, you, the recipient, are treated like service doesn't count.

A few months ago I ordered a new treadmill and was told that the delivery charge and set up fee would be around $175. It sounded pricey but I was in no position to pick it up myself, carry it into the house and set it up properly. It seemed the store and the delivery people knew this so it gave them a reason to take advantage.

I was asked if I would like a morning or afternoon delivery, which meant a four-hour window that would require me to take off from work and spend the day waiting until they were good and ready to show up.

My first thought was, "Wait a minute. I'm the customer. Don't I have a say in this process?" After all, I was the one paying for this service and losing four hours of work. This now made the service cost almost triple, if I factored in my time.

I told the sales department that I needed a more specific time frame and, even though the salesperson was dying to get the commission, he told me there was nothing he could do. I would get a call the night before to confirm, so I had better call in absent from work and get ready to wait.

Finally, the big day came for my morning delivery. I sat and sat some more, and by the time the morning ended, no one had shown up. The only thing I could do was call the store and inquire about the delivery. They gave me a number for the delivery company so I called and rescheduled my appointment. Naturally, when I asked what had happened the first time, they played dumb and said that the delivery people were just running behind. The fact that I was paying the bill and wasting my time meant nothing to them.

I scheduled another date for delivery and stated that if they didn't show during the appointed time, they shouldn't bother coming. The second window came and went and there was still no delivery during my morning timeframe. I finally left for the office and as I was pulling out of my driveway, guess who came pulling up with the delivery?

Most people would have been glad to see them, gotten out of their car and hung around while the unit was delivered and set up. But I was so tired of being taken advantage of that I walked up to the drivers and told them that they missed the delivery window so they could just take the equipment back to the warehouse. Think they cared? Absolutely not. These were workers, not owners, so it didn't matter to them.

The next day I went to the store to ask for my credit and they didn't even try to talk me out of it. People just don't care about the companies they work for since, at the end of the day, they go home with a paycheck while the owners have to worry about why the sales revenue is declining. There are many stores that end up in financial trouble or even go bankrupt; it has nothing to do with the cost of goods but is directly related to poor customer service.

Case Four: Managerial Mismanagement

If you've ever gone into one of those large home goods or electronic box stores to buy something, you know how easy it is for them to quickly take your money and get you out of there. Just try to do a return and see what happens.

I arrive at the store a week later with my return item and receipt in hand. The first thing I am greeted with is a long line, all doing returns or exchanges. There may be two employees handling returns, but it often takes both of them to do one successfully. They consult with each other at the counter while, all that time, I wait and wait. And the managers are nowhere to be found. Should I simply wait?

I usually take an active role and ask the person behind me to hold my place in line while I go get a manager. Many times I am successful and ask the managers what they notice about their customers in line. All too often the manager plays stupid and says nothing. Then I point out the fact that there are fifteen people in line and only two people doing returns, both of whom have no idea what they are doing.

In some stores, the manager will get someone else involved to help but in the two types of stores that I mentioned, they usually simply respond that there aren't enough employees at that time and walk away. Wouldn't you think that if the manager is concerned for the success of his or her store, he or she would fill in when short-handed? But many managers will not 'lower' themselves to the level of having to talk with customers. They stay in their little ivory tower office and do nothing but direct the head cashier or the manager of the day to handle the problem. These people aren't interested in their store, their jobs, or the customers who shop there. All they want is a paycheck.

One of the things I will do if the manager refuses to talk is call the 800-number posted on the signs while I wait there in line. When I get done with the customer service department, a manager often shows up and asks, "Who just called?" They have had to leave their office and are forced to talk with me under corporate instructions.

I use every form of ingenuity to accomplish my goal and get a response—and a return.

Chapter 17

Taking on the Cruise Lines

Have you ever taken a cruise? They are supposed to be enjoyable and relaxing—and in the past, they used to be. But since there are now so many different ships and cruise lines, what was once an industry offering friendly, courteous service has changed into a business of getting us on board and then getting us off to make room for new passengers. Everything is based on profits. Even though most employees involved in the cruise industry still seem nice, when the going gets tough, you'll realize how hard it is to find a port in the storm.

Cruise lines will gladly take your money and promise you the world. But let there be some problem and they'd turn it around to seem like your fault and try to make you feel guilty of something. We consumers are lucky they can't make us walk the plank!

Case One: A Rotten Room

A few years ago, we decided to take a last-minute cruise in the Caribbean on one of those famous large ships and ended up booking an outside room with an obstructed view. It didn't matter; this was our ninth cruise and we tend to spend very little time in the room anyway. Between being on shore or out and about on the ship most of the day, the room becomes little more than a place to change and sleep.

We boarded the ship and it was truly beautiful. The room was as expected, with a view of the lifeboats. The only initial problem was that we had to keep the curtains closed since the crew was often walking around outside our windows, but that didn't bother us.

We set sail and all was well. On the first night, we partied until the early hours of the next morning, figuring we could sleep late. Wrong. The crew was up at about 5 a.m., pressure-washing the boat outside our window. We had only gotten about three and a half hours of sleep. What a way to relax!

I got dressed and went to the purser's office to complain and see if something could be done to discontinue the early morning cleaning. The young officer (more like a front desk clerk) said he'd see what he could do, which was basically nothing. The noise didn't stop so later that same morning I went to the hotel manager to explain the situation.

Instead of having a nice, helpful attitude, this manager was belligerent from the start. His primary position was that he ran the hotel portion of the cruise and that my problem was with the captain's portion. He couldn't see any way he could help so I asked for another room. Naturally, the corporate office instructs them to never offer another room, under any circumstance. He replied that the ship was full, so I asked my cleaning person to let me know if there were any empty rooms. Turns out there were plenty.

What could we do? There we were, out at sea, so it wasn't as if we could simply vacate our room and move to another hotel. We were captives of the cruise line.

The next morning came and the same thing happened. Now I was getting really steamed. I went to find the hotel manager's room (since I knew he wasn't below with the other crew), but luckily for him I couldn't find it. If I did, I would have pounded on his door at 3 a.m. to wake him.

The next day, one of the tenders could not be unloaded from the ship because some mechanism was broken. The crew decided to remove it and put it in another cleat. The equipment was placed…where else? Outside our window! It consisted of an acetylene tank and an oxygen tank. Tanks are quiet, I thought, so no problem...until that night. We encountered high seas and though the crew was nowhere to be found, the tanks were rolling around on the catwalk outside our window. Being in a field that uses oxygen tanks, I knew that they were required to be strapped down or locked to the wall. If a valve is broken or a spark occurs from friction, that tank could act like a torpedo and shoot through a window or even the side of the ship. And we were supposed to sleep in the room with the tanks just outside.

I went to the purser right then and explained the whole situation; he turned a deaf ear and refused to do anything. I was fuming at this point and didn't want to go to bed in that room. We were thinking of sleeping in the lounge area all night in hopes that the tanks would be removed the next day. This is what I did instead.

I contacted the operator and declared an emergency, insisting to see the captain immediately. The primary captain was asleep so I told her to wake him, which I knew she was not going to do. So the operator put me in touch with the front desk clerk, who asked me to explain the problem. I refused to discuss it until the captain or someone in command was available to come to my room and meet with me. But the desk clerk tried his best not to produce any of the captains.

I decided to tell him that the safety of the ship was in question and that there was the potential for a fire or damage to the ship if someone didn't get to my room immediately.

This caught their attention. The first officer came to my room with one of the pursers. I explained the problem and the potential danger to the ship, my person and my family. The officer looked outside the window and saw the problem so he immediately radioed for the crew to get up to the catwalk and remove everything. If I hadn't stood up for myself in this situation, there could have been a serious accident.

At this point, a good part of my trip had been ruined by that dangerous situation and by the early morning noise of the crew cleaning. We were in the middle of nowhere so I had no choice but to stay on the ship, but when I got home, all hell would break loose!

The average consumer would consider it a bad experience and move on, and the cruise line would go on its merry way, not knowing how wrong things were in the first place since it's unlikely that anyone would have reported it to corporate. Therefore, there would be zero chance of improvement.

I really wanted to stand up for myself, stop suffering through bad service and make a change, so I wrote a detailed letter to the customer service division and "cc"ed my attorney.

I put every little detail in the letter and made sure to let them know how my vacation was ruined by stress (I told them how afraid my wife and I were of having to stay in that room and that we seriously considered sleeping on lounge chairs instead). Don't be afraid to ask for a free cruise to make up for that stress and for putting you in such a bad situation. Even though these ships are registered outside the United States, that doesn't mean they are not subject to U.S. maritime regulations.

I completed my letter and sent it through certified mail, then did nothing but wait. At first I received a computer-generated notice acknowledging the receipt of my letter. It took almost four months for the corporate office to investigate the entire situation, and finally I received a *real* letter of apology saying there was no way to make up for my inconvenience. As a gesture of good will, the cruise line gave me one year to book another cruise with them at the best deal I could find and I'd receive half off the price per person.

The next cruise my wife and I took cost a total of just $750 for the two of us.

Case 2: Stolen Property

What a wonderful time we were going to have cruising from Venice to other parts of the world. I brought my new iPod with me on board so I could listen to music while reading, exercising or just sitting around. I had also bought all of the appropriate insurance policies recommended by the cruise line, through their own program, to cover everything from a trip cancellation to lost baggage, delay and so on. I thought it was well worth the money since the cruise line makes all types of promises about these policies and how necessary they are to have peace of mind from the day I set sail until I arrive home.

During the third day on the cruise, we were in port and I was about to leave for our land tour. All valuables were locked in the room safe, which couldn't be any smaller. It barely held my wallet, let alone all of our jewelry.

As we were leaving the ship, I noticed that some of the doors to the rooms were wide open. I questioned the cabin steward only to find out that the cruise line had ordered new deck furniture for each room and it was going to be placed on every deck while we were in port. I was assured that only one room had to be opened and everything would be carried to the outside deck doors through only one cabin.

After a few hours on land we returned to our room to rest before dinner. I wanted to relax with some music and noticed that my earphones were sitting on the night table but my iPod was missing. My first thought was that I misplaced it so I did a thorough search of the cabin, under the furniture and beds and even in the safe, but nothing turned up. Other than our cabin steward, no one was in the room, we thought.

I went to the purser's desk to report the possible theft. The first step was to notify the head steward, our steward, and the head purser. Everyone came to our room to do a thorough search. No stone was left unturned by the crew but, still, the iPod was missing.

This is when you think the ship's cruising agreement or your insurance would help in such as situation. Think again. And definitely think twice about buying this coverage.

I had to fill out a loss report with the head purser to be sent to the corporate office in the United States. (Look carefully at what you are signing. The cruise line, like so many other large companies, was trying to dupe me into signing something I shouldn't.)

The form required me to fill out the ship name, my name and address, etc., etc. Finally it required my signature before the purser would sign it and forward it to corporate. The statement I was to sign was that this was a mysterious disappearance of my property and I was indemnifying the cruise line from any damages. The desk purser said I must sign it, but I refused. I asked to see the head purser, who sent back word that he would not sign the form unless I signed it first.

That was the time for any prudent person to either get tough or acquiesce. My feathers were ruffled so I told the purser to stop running back and forth with messages from the head purser. I politely asked him to tell the head purser to get off his lazy ass and come out to talk with me directly. If he did not, I intended to find the captain and report a theft by one of the crewmembers directly to him.

This brought the head purser flying over, saying he could not send the report without my signature. I said I would sign only if the statement about indemnifying the cruise liner was crossed out first. Again he insisted he would not sign until I accepted the statement. In situations like these, I recommend that, for your own good, you don't back down. If you do, you may give up your rights, which are the only things that may help you in the end.

I crossed out the statement myself and signed. Then I told the head purser to sign and file it immediately after he gave me a copy, reminding him that my reporting a theft to the captain would create a much larger problem. He signed and gave me a copy, and I watched as he faxed the report back to corporate headquarters in the U.S.

Furthermore, on a new ship like this, I insisted they pull the lock record (every time guests go into their rooms on a ship or even in a newer hotel, their use of the magnetic swipe "key" card is registered in an electronic record). Sure enough, it indicated the three times I used my key, but it also showed that the cabin steward used his key not just once in the morning while cleaning the room, but also in the mid-afternoon, when it recorded that the door had been left open for quite some time.

That meant that either the steward opened the door and walked away, giving someone else the chance to wander in and take the iPod, or the crew changing the chairs on the decks went through my room.

I called my steward and for a few bucks, he talked. The chairs for the balcony were too large to bring in from the outside so they had to bring them in through every room, which is why the doors were opened. It seemed obvious then that one of the crew had ripped me off.

I relayed this story to the purser, who told me he'd look into it. Two hours later, the head cabin steward called to say that my steward had given me wrong information. I could smell a cover-up! They didn't want the passengers knowing their doors had been left wide open, especially when we had been assured that they wouldn't be.

The next thing I noticed was that the cabin steward was no longer working on our floor, which meant they either fired him or made him stay away for the rest of the trip. There are no labor laws when it comes to cruise lines.

Okay, so the cruise ended—but the real fun began when I came home and had to file a claim with the cruise line and the insurance company. I started this recovery process as soon as I got back to the U.S., but it wasn't easy. Let me tell you that cruise lines and insurance companies will run you around in circles, hoping you will simply give up.

But I was ready for battle! I contacted the corporate

office of the cruise line first. After being routed around to different offices, I finally made contact with the one that handles these types of issues. Of course, that doesn't mean I actually *spoke* to anyone! I got a message that went something like this: "Your call is important to us so please leave your name and number and one of our representatives will get back to you within two business days." So I left a number and waited.

Naturally, the call came the moment I was away from the phone, so they left me the original number to call again. (I'm still trying to figure out how they do that. Maybe all consumers have a magnetic swipe in our heads that records when we leave the house and all companies have access to this information!) So then I had to get rerouted to the proper office again, only to receive that same message. This game of telephone tag can go on forever if you don't sit by the phone 24/7.

Here's how to win that game. Instead of leaving a message, I started the call over again and chose some other office to complain to. It may not work the first time since often that person will ask me to hold and simply transfer me to the number I didn't want to reach in the first place. I just keep calling back until someone listens and takes charge. I can often get through to a live person in the appropriate office—*with* the help of someone else inside the corporate system.

I explained my problem and was told to file a claim form and send it to their office for review. What does this "review" actually entail? Well, it's a way for them to delay making payment. But I did as I was told and after about six weeks, I called to see what was happening. Nothing! They said it would take *another* six weeks. My best course of action at this point was to raise a dispute with my credit card company over the balance due the cruise line until I got some action.

Finally, six more weeks passed and I received a letter, with all my material returned, telling me I needed to apply to the insurance company for reimbursement. The cruise line also sent a statement from their contract showing me exactly why they would not be held subject to payment (even though that same contract did state a form of liability). Of course, this is open to interpretation, which differs according to who is reading the statement.

I now had to start again by calling the insurance company and downloading their claim form. Fortunately, I had copies of all my documentation. When unsure, send them more than they ask for, anything that applies, even if it is minutiae.

After only five more weeks of waiting, I received notice that the insurance company had just gotten my material and it would take four to six weeks for processing. I guess the process really starts when someone finally gets around to dusting off and opening an envelope that has been sitting on a desk for weeks. In the meantime, I was still disputing all my on-board charges with the cruise line since someone had to pay for my missing belonging.

At this point, I had two choices: wait and continue to play their game or contact the insurance commissioner in my state. I chose the latter and filed a complaint form stating that my insurance company was doing everything in its power not to pay my claim.

That must have worked because, two and a half weeks later, I received a check from the insurance company with a ten percent depreciation. My iPod was only nine months old so I immediately called them and complained that this was not acceptable. They referred to the fine print in the policy. But do you think I've ever let a little fine print stop me?

I filed a subsequent claim for the cost of the iPod case and all the music I had downloaded. The insurance company would not cover the full cost of all the music stored but they offered a settlement of eighty percent on it and I agreed. It made up for the ten percent they withheld plus gave me some extra funds to purchase a newer, upgraded iPod.

The point of this story is not to give up and allow a large insurance company to have the upper hand. You, the consumer, will win in most cases—*if* you know how to use the system to your benefit. I had purchased the cruise line's insurance policy, which came with many promises, and I intended to make them keep those promises. And you can, too, which should be music to your ears.

Case Three: Cruise Changes

Everyone in the travel industry, especially in the cruise lines, is out there selling you a dream. They tell you how wonderful their trips are and that if you book early, you can receive extra discounts. So, after careful thought, you chose your cruise and prepay, knowing that you have just saved some money for booking early. What you don't expect is for the cruise line to change your cruise at its discretion. Well, that's what happened to me.

The cruise was eleven months away but we booked all of our air travel to and from Europe, the tickets we'd need while there, and our hotel reservations for before and after we set sail. Everything was taken care of.

A month went by and we got a call from our travel agent informing us that the cruise line cancelled our trip and wanted us to reschedule a different date, reverse our itinerary, or get a refund. I couldn't believe that they could just cancel our trip like that, so I read the contract of passage, which gave them the right to cancel if the cruise line sold the ship to a charter. They retain this right almost up to the day the trip begins.

To entice us to reverse our itinerary, they told the travel agent they'd upgrade our room, not to a suite but to a deck just one above our original booking. This really didn't mean anything since the room was the same size and configuration. What did matter, however, was what it would cost us to change all of our air travel arrangements. Moving us one deck higher would not make up for that!

Unwilling to accept the cruise line's mediocre offering, I decided to look on the Internet for the U.S. rules of passage (although this cruise was operating in Europe, the corporate offices were in the United States.) These rules were quite clear. Although the tour operator wrote into their contract that they have the right to cancel if something better came along, the federal rules indicated otherwise.

I contacted my travel agent, who really wasn't versed in these rules and had no idea how to handle the situation. Her office only knew how to book trips, but when a problem arose, they were at a loss in helping their clients. I asked her to contact the cruise tour operator to talk with me directly. They normally don't want to speak to anyone but the travel agent, but since I was prepared to take legal action against the tour operator, it would be in her best interest to deal with me.

Two days went by and I did receive a call from someone representing the cruise tour operator's customer service department. She offered me the same deal as before but this time agreed to pay the fees for the airline changes. I still wasn't happy with the situation so I decided to push for a deeper discount. She immediately responded that it wasn't going to happen, but that she would gladly give me back my deposit (what would be the point if I'd lose the cost of the airfare?). Up to then, the conversation was very polite, but we were simply playing cat and mouse.

Rather than give up, I decided to push a little harder, but still in a polite way. When I explained the federal guidelines that her cruise line had to follow, she became flustered and was at a loss for words. Now was the time to tell her what I wanted in return for this inconvenience. (During negotiation, it is very important to know what you want and when to ask for it. The worst they could say is no...but sometimes they will say yes!)

I said I wanted a two-for-one discount, which cruise lines often offer near the departure date in order to sell off any remaining rooms. This was a very expensive trip but I was assuming the responsibility of handling the changes in my travel and hotel arrangements myself. My tone had become a little more forceful, so the cruise tour operator understood that I meant business. But just to make sure, I explained that if I had to cancel and lose the airfare, I was prepared to take the company to court, which, win or lose, would cost them a lot in legal fees. She said she'd have to talk with corporate and get back to me in a couple of days.

Exactly two days later, I got the call that the corporate office agreed to my request and was only going to charge me fifty percent of the total cost for the cruise. Their only stipulation was that I not tell anybody on the ship so that it wouldn't present further problems for them.

The bottom line is that had I been weak and accepted their early offer, it would have cost me around $600 to change my airline arrangements. Through negotiation and spelling out exactly what I wanted, I ended up saving over $5,000 for my trip and only spent $250 to change my flights.

Consumers have become programmed to accept being inconvenienced and shortchanged. I say, why make it easy for these companies to do that to you? Especially when we've got the weapons to fight back!

Conclusion

I hope that by reading this book, you have gotten the feeling that things don't always have to remain status quo. What I have learned is that the bigger the company, the more complacent they become and the more comfortable they feel taking advantage of consumers. I guess they think that there is nothing one little person can do about it. It's time to make them think again.

Don't be afraid to stand up for your rights. At this point, you should have all gotten a sense of the steps that may be necessary to get these businesses to recognize you as a person, not just a credit card number purchasing their products or services. If you are not sure about what to do, ask someone (such as a local court clerk) for an opinion before you launch your offense—and remember that sometimes a good offense is really your best line of defense.

The more people who take the time to get involved, rather than accepting defeat, the more companies or service organizations will start to take notice. These companies are happy to sell us a good or service and must be held accountable for their promises and guarantees, no matter if they are written or implied. Force their customer service departments to be more than just a phone answering service that always apologizes, rather than actually fixing the problem. Using the proper dialogue at the right time, even if it is caustic, will often get someone moving in the direction you want.

Use every available resource, including the legal system, insurance commissions, government agencies, compliance groups, etc., that is at your disposal. Sure, we all work and feel that we do not have the time or the know-how to take on big business, but in the end, it is well worth it.

You are the consumer or customer and without you, these companies or agencies would not exist, so go for it and make them own up to their promises. We will all benefit from your actions, but no one ever benefits from a lack of action—except the companies themselves. The more people get involved, the better it will be for all of us down the road. If ten consumers are taken advantage of in the same way by a company and only one speaks up, the company will continue to do business as usual. If, on the other hand, eight of the ten people speak up, the company will change the way it operates because it can't afford to anger too many people or lose that many customers. It is just bad for business.